MILITIAE

Panzerkampfwagen IV
The Wehrmacht´s armoured fist

Carlos Caballero Jurado
Lucas Molina Franco

AF EDITIONS

CHAPTER I

ORIGINS AND DEVELOPMENT OF THE TANK

There are words that nobody tries to translate into their own language. In the military field, these are words like guerrilla, marine or panzer. Everybody just knows, for instance, the meaning of 'panzer'. And this is because the German Armoured Arm, the *Panzerwaffe*, is still regarded as the best-armoured corps in history. Such is their fame that we often forget that they were actually a small number of men. In order to give an idea, it is worth mentioning specific data. By October 1943 the German Army had twenty-two panzer divisions, with a total of 288,000 men. But in the panzer regiments in them (one per division) and other independent panzer units of smaller size, the total personnel were roughly 22,000 men, a tiny amount as compared to the total of soldiers serving the German Army. The fact that there were also some panzer troops in the *Waffen SS* and even armoured units of the *Luftwaffe* by the time does not change the main picture.

Among the vehicles serving the *Panzerwaffe*, none of them did so in amounts comparable to the *Panzer* IV or –to use the official designation– the *Panzerkampfwagen* IV (Sd.Kfz. 161). At nearly 8,600 delivered to the German Armed Forces (*Wehrmacht*), the *Panzer* IV surpasses by far the figures of German tanks of any other type in service. To round up the figures, it should be noticed that the *Wehrmacht* was supplied with 6,100 *Panzer* IIIs, 6,000 *Panzer* V *Panthers*, 1,800 *Panzer* IIs, 1,800 *Panzer* VI *Tigers* (in two versions), 1,500 *Panzer* Is and 1,400 *Panzer* 38(t)s and we have already mentioned the *Panzer* IV figures. This means that the *Panzer* IV alone represented more than thirty per cent of the tanks turned out by German factories or under their control that served in the *Wehrmacht*.

On the other hand, other armoured vehicles were built for very different roles using the *Panzer* IV hulls, assault guns (*Sturmgeschütz* IV and *Sturmpanzer* IV *Brumbär*), anti-tank self-propelled guns (*Nashorn*), tank destroyers (*Jagdpanzer* IV), self-propelled field guns (*Hummel*) and self-propelled anti-aircraft tanks (*Möbelwagen*, *Wirbeldwind*, *Ostwind*). The numbers of vehicles of all the types mentioned above built makes a total of another 5,000 armoured vehicles that served the *Wehrmacht* and stemmed from the *Panzer* IV.

Many other concepts developed from the *Panzer* IV did not go beyond the drawing boards, remained in the stage of test prototypes or were produced in irrelevant amounts. Just mentioning them all would require a lot of space. But I cannot resist stopping at one of them, the device that was officially named as the 10,5-cm K18 *auf Panzer selbstfahrlafette* IV a (10.5 K18 Gun Motor Carriage IV a). It was a 105-mm self-propelled field gun that, contrary to what was later to become common among the German tanks, was totally and heavily armoured, as it was designed with a very defined goal in mind: to beat very powerful enemy fortifications from the shortest distance possible, a moving blockhouse that should smash static concrete bunkers. Those bunkers that they were designed to beat were no other than Gibraltar's. The *Panzer* IV hull was chosen because it was the only one that was able to stand the weight of the gun along with the heavy armour required. The two tanks built were shown to Hitler in the spring of 1941, but by then, obsessed as he was with the intended offensive on the USSR, the *Führer* had lost the little interest he ever had had concerning Gibraltar, so, after praising the beast, he ordered to study the feasibility of its production as a tank destroyer. That was the end of the project because, although the two built were used for that task in the summer of 1941 proving exceptionally efficient, it was an extremely expensive arms system to be produced in the large scale the tank destroyers were needed. I could not resist telling this story because, as far as I know, I think it is the only German armoured device specifically conceived to be used on Spanish soil.

Turning back to the *Panzer* IV properly, the fist striking thing is that it was the only German tank whose production started before the Second World War and kept on rolling off the factories until the end of the war, although, naturally, the last to be built, the J version, were very different from the original A version. Nevertheless, this would have been impossible but for the fact that it was a really good design from the start, for this was the characteristic that allowed introducing subsequent improvements. Germany entered the war with the tanks of the first panzer generation (the *Panzer* I to *Panzer* IV types), which very soon proved obsolete. The conflict had already started when the second generation of *panzers* (the magnificent *Panthers* and *Tigers*) was designed, but their operational phase-in took a long time. It was the *Panzer*

3

IV that filled in the gap between both generations, as it was the only one of the first generation to be suitably perfected.

So far all that has been said here seems to lead to the conclusion that, from the beginning of the war to the end the German plan makers assigned a main role to the *Panzer* IV, whereas it is quite different. Until the summer of 1941 the Germans still believed that the tandem made up by the *Panzer* II and the *Panzer* III would be enough for the *Panzerwaffe* to fulfil the tasks assigned in the *Blitzkrieg*. This illusion faded as the Soviet T-34 and KV tanks were first met, just at the start of the Russian campaign. For a long time, the *Panzer* IV was the only response that the Germans managed to oppose to the new danger.

In the face of the unexpected Russian challenge, the Germans started to work –by late 1941– on what were to be the *Panther* and the *Tiger*. Both the engineers and the tank crews were so fascinated with these two war beasts that it was even thought of cancelling the production of all other armoured vehicles to concentrate exclusively on one of these two types. But the task of designing, starting production and then ironing out the innumerable problems posed by a new tank (especially if they were as sophisticated as the *Panther* and the *Tiger* were), inevitably took a very long time. So it certainly was not possible to do without the production of the *Panzer* IV, otherwise the Panzerwaffe would have been left with just a handful of tanks and, as a matter of fact, it was on them that the weight of the armoured war fell on for many months. Summing up, the main role of the *Panzer* IV in the history of the *Panzerwaffe* was never that intended for it, neither by the tank crews nor by the engineers. But that was the role it eventually played.

This explains the surprisingly low figures of the *Panzer* IVs built before the war and even during the early war years. By late 1938, 115 been delivered, in 1939, the year of the outbreak of the Second World War, only a further 141 were produced. In 1940 the number was 278, and 467 rolled off the factories in 1941. So far, all the figures correspond to different versions armed with the 75 mm short-barrel gun. In order to face the unexpected T-34s and KVs, the *Panzer* IV had to be fitted with a 75 mm long-barrel gun, and now –as a matter of fact, converted into the main battle tank of the *Wehrmacht*– production multiplied. Thus, 1,019 were delivered in

1942 (only 124 were fitted with the short gun). In 1943 and 1944 the figures of *Panzer* IVs built (3,013 and 3,126 respectively) were three as many as those delivered in 1942 and six as many as those produced in 1941. And that despite the fact that, by then, the circumstances Germany was facing were much more adverse. In other words, the 3,000 figures should have been achieved by 1940 or 1941. If so, the *Wehrmacht* would have been able to face campaigns like that of Russia from a much more advantageous position. I will not make the mistake of stating that, should the 3rd *Reich* had had a few hundred *Panzer* IVs more by that time, it would have managed to win the war, because a conflict of the size of the Second World War is something utterly complex. But it is indeed correct and realistic to state that the result of quite a few battles –and maybe even of some campaigns as a whole– might have been different if by June 1941, instead of attacking the USSR with an armour inventory made up essentially of 1,500 *Panzer* IIIs, 1,000 *Panzer* IIs and just 500 *Panzer* IVs, the latter had been say 2,000 for instance.

By putting it in that way, it may seem that German strategists and technicians were quite stupid. But that was not the case. In 1939, by the outbreak of the Second World War, the future of the armour war was an enigma. Theories strived but they were just that, theory. And there were for all tastes at that. What characteristics the main tank should have? How should the tank units be organized at different levels? How many models or types of tanks were necessary to carry out the various tasks? Which tactics were the most suitable? Each question could have many answers.

The German Army thought that there was a need for a tank armed with heavy machine guns, able to attack the enemy infantry and artillery, the *Panzer* II (with one 20-mm and one 7.92-mm machine gun) and a tank able to fight enemy tanks, the *Panzer* III, which should be fitted with an initial high-speed 37 or 50-mm gun and piercing ammunition. The *Panzer* I was always seen as an interim solution, apt for crew training, necessary only until the German industry (for which the Treaty of Versailles had put a ban on the construction of tanks) was in condition to produce sufficient numbers of *Panzer* IIs and *Panzer* IIIs. As the German industry encountered more problems than expected for the mass production of tanks, the *Wehrmacht* introduced into its inventory large numbers of Czech *Panzer* 35(t) and *Panzer* 38(t) tanks. But this was also seen as a temporary solution. Given the background, which was the role reserved for the *Panzer* IV?

The *Panzer* IV was conceived as an "escort vehicle", a *Begleitpanzerwagen*, which should accompany the *Panzer* II and *Panzer* III and whose short 75-mm gun, basically with high-explosive ammunition, would be tasked with suppressing what was already foreseen as one of the great enemies of the tank, the anti-tank gun, or else enemy fortifications. The *Begleitpanzerwagen*, the future *Panzer* IV, was thus born to supplement the MG-*Panzerwagen* (Machinegun Armoured Vehicle), the *Panzer* II and the *Geschützpanzerwagen* (Gun-armed Tank), the *Panzer* III. This explains the fact that the differences between the basic characteristics of the *Panzer* III and the *Panzer* IV are much less important than the very great ones existing between the *Panzer* II and the *Panzer* III.

Seen from the current perspective, the decision of making the *Panzer* IV an almost ancillary element in the armour inventory instead of the main battle tank might seem a serious mistake and maybe it actually was. And though one should not forgive that, in the last instance the *Panzer* II and *Panzer* III duo gave Germany considerable victories. In that case, the calculation on which their existence was based cannot be considered crazy.

The similarities between the *Panzer* III and *Panzer* IV were so remarkable that by the end of the summer of 1941, there were plans to create a "mixed" type, provisionally baptized as the *Panzer* III/IV, of which some prototypes were produced before the idea was rejected. But there are more examples of the basic similitude between both types. For instance, the *Sturmgeschütz* IV assault guns were basically superstructures of the *Sturmgeschütz* III (originally thought for the *Panzer* III hulls) mounted on the *Panzer* IV hulls. On the other hand, the *Nashorn* self-propelled anti-tank gun and the *Hummel* self-propelled field gun combined the *Panzer* IV hulls they were mounted on with the propulsion of the *Panzer* III moving them.

Getting back to the origin of the *Panzer* IV, i.e. early 1934, when the German Army asked the industry for a *Begleitpanzerwa-*

A wooden mock-up of the project devised by Krupp in response to the request for the *Begleitpanzerwagen*.

gen to supplement the *Panzer* II and *Panzer* III. The Rheinmetall-Borsig, MAN and Krupp companies presented their projects and the Krupp design was finally chosen. Krupp always remained the main contractor, although from the F version on other great companies, the Vomag and the Nibelungswerke also built these tanks. Essentially, and despite the numerous versions and adaptations, the original Krupp design remained unchanged.

The running gear was made up of a front driving sprocket wheel, a rear idler wheel, four bogies of two road wheels each, leaf spring suspension and four return rollers. The gasoline V 12-cylinder Maybach engine, placed in the rear, was made by the company that built practically all the engines for all the German tanks. In the A version (*Ausführung A, Ausf A*), the engine type was the 250-hp HL 108 TR. All of the later versions though were fitted with the 320-hp HL 120 TR type. In the same way, whereas the *Ausf A* had a ZF five-front and one rear gear SGR 75 transmission, the later versions had a six-front and one rear gear SSG 75 gearbox. If the A version had a top speed of 31 kph and a 150 km top range, the propulsion of the other versions increased top speed to 40 kph and range to up to 200 km (road, in both cases). The off-road top speed was 20 kph and maximum range was 130 km. These characteristics were downgraded as the weight of the different versions increased. The off-road performances were acceptable, maximum vertical obstacle was 0.6 m and 2.3-m ditches. Maximum fording depth was 0.8 m and it could climb slopes up to 30° (and higher slopes but with greater difficulty).

The very roomy turret was one of the great achievements of the tank; it housed the main armament, the gun, and most of the crew. Thanks to its size, it could later be fitted with much heavier armament than the original. The tank commander was in the centre,

Krupp also designed this tank prototype, very similar to the future *Panzer* IV, conceived for export but never built.

under a cupola of excellent design and affording good vision over the ground. The loader and gunner sat left and right of the gun respectively. Both of them had their respective side hatches for entry and exit. The turret was powered by an auxiliary motor, and could thus turn fast (although in case of need it could be operated by hand). In most versions, and certainly in those built in large numbers, a container was added in the rear of the turret for the crew's personal objects, which made a longer profile.

The other two crewmen, the driver and the radio operator (who doubled as gunner in the hull) were housed left and right of the driver's compartment. They also had their own access hatches, in this case in the upper part of the superstructure.

The armament was made up of a gun and machine guns. As regards the latter, there were two 7.92-mm MG-13s in the A version, one coaxial to the gun and the other in the hull. The B version was fitted with an MG-34 (also of 7.92 calibre), but in this case the tank had only the coaxial one, a characteristic that was retained in the C version. The D version saw the return of two machine guns, which was kept to the latest types. As we have said, the *Panzer* IV was originally fitted with short-barrelled 75-mm gun, namely the *Kampfwagenkanone* 37 L/24 (KwK 37 L/24; Type 37 tank gun of 24 calibres), with low muzzle velocity and thought to fire in curve trajectories, basically high-explosive ammuni-

tion. This gun was fitted to the A through the F versions, although the final change was introduced with the 75-mm long-barrelled gun while the latter was in production, but we shall see this later (some tanks of the D version were rebuilt to accommodate 75-mm long-barrelled guns).

Armour on the *Ausf A* was only 15 mm, which could barely stand very light antitank gun shells and shrapnel. Front armour was already thickened in the *Ausf B* to 30 mm, although 15 mm of armour was maintained in the sides and rear. The first version to see service use once the war had broken out, the *Ausf D*, had side and rear armour increased to 20 mm. As we shall see later, armour was progressively increased in the new versions, as an answer to a growingly lethal battlefield.

In order to understand the new changes appearing in the new versions, it is necessary to deal with both the campaigns taking place and the changes in the organic structure of the panzer troops.

Only thirty-five tanks of the first version, the *Ausf A*, were produced and delivered from October to March 1938. After the conclusion of the French campaign, they were seen so obsolete that those still operational were relegated to training tasks. The *Ausf B* was also built in ridiculously small numbers, forty-two. From late 1940 onwards, side armour was reinforced with additional bolted plates, which allowed it to remain operational until 1943, when the last ones were struck off charge. The C ver-

A *Panzer IV Ausf A* on a wading test. In order to overcome the ever-slippery banks, firewood bundles have been placed under it. .

Foto: Bundesarchiv 146-1978-120-15

sion was the last produced before the war, from September 1938 to August 1939. Although 300 of this series were ordered, only 134 were ever produced. As in the previous case, they served until 1943 when they finally vanished from the German armoured inventory.

The Order of Battle (OB) of the pre-war armoured battalions established a structure with a staff company (*Stab Panzer Kompanie*), two light companies (*leichte Panzer Kompanie*) and a so-called "A" light company, leichte *Pz. Kp.* (a) which should be transformed in due time, as sufficient numbers of tanks became available, into a medium company (*mittlere Panzer Kompanie*). Those interim "A" light companies had twenty-two tanks on strength, of the *Panzer* I, II, III and *Panzer* IV types, a real hotchpotch. As the number of *Panzer* IVs was so small, in the 1937 OB they had only four *Panzer* IVs each, and in 1939 the figure rose to six. Shortly before the Polish campaign, the first *mittlere Panzer Kompanie* were officially established, each to be equipped with fourteen *Panzer* IVs and five *Panzer* IIs. But the war broke out and only two of the German armoured battalions had these medium companies, whereas the rest still had the "A" companies (and some of them still with four *Panzer* IVs...).

The Polish campaign evidenced the limitations of the *Panzerwaffe* such as it was equipped. On 1 September 1939 the German armoured troops had 1,445 Panzer Is, 1,223 *Panzer* IIs, 202 *Panzer* 35(t)s, 98 *Panzer* IIIs and 78 *Panzer* 38(t)s. As regards the *Panzer* IV, there were 211 in service, of which 197 were allotted to combat units, eleven to training units and three to arsenals. Unfairly, the Polish campaign is often underestimated in the books about the Second World War. The Polish Army certainly fought so bravely and with such remarkable ability (with much more ability than that shown later by the British and the French) and though their extremely limited armoured arms were no enemy to the *Panzerwaffe*, that cannot be applied to their anti-tank arms, which caused serious losses among the German tank ranks. It soon proved, for instance, that the *Panzer* IV armour was too weak and, as we have said, it was reinforced in the first version ordered after the start of the war, the D version. Another experience gained from the Polish campaign was that of the inefficiency of the "A" companies, as the tanks of those units had extre-

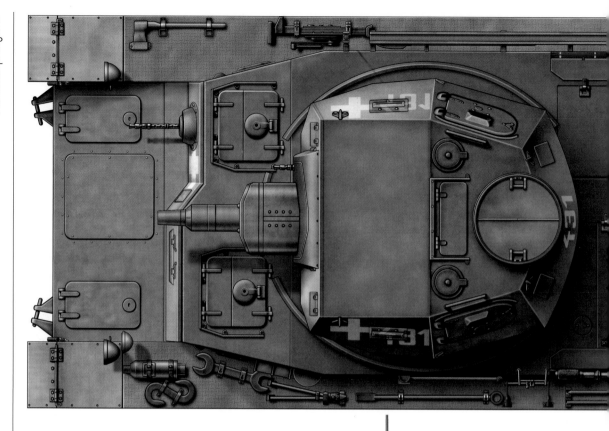

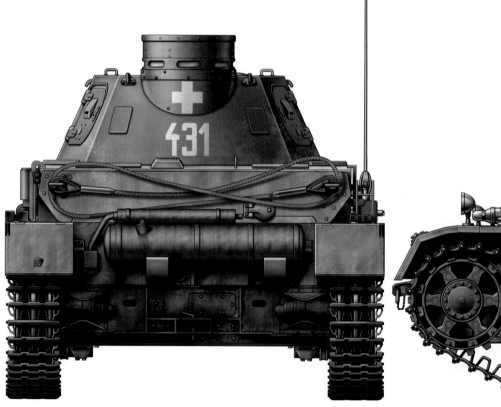

mely different technical features and tactical capacities. Thus orders were issued to extend the type medium company as fast as possible in all the armoured battalions, but as there were so few *Panzer* IVs available, the numbers of these tanks in each unit shrank to eight.

The D version had been ordered in January 1938, with a total of 248, but deliveries started in October 1939 and it was built until May 1941, totalling 229 built. A few of them took part in the Western campaign in May 1940. However, by that date too, the German armoured inventory was essentially made up of much more lightly armoured tanks, 1,077 *Panzer* Is, 1,092 *Panzer* IIs, 381 *Panzer* IIIs, 248 *Panzer* 38(t)s and 143 *Panzer* 35(t)s. The *Panzer* IVs amounted to an as little impressive figure as 290. Even so, the *Panzerwaffe* was able to play its role brilliantly, smashing the Franco-British armoured forces, which enjoyed a larger number of tanks, most of which were better armed and had heavier armour. Thus, the victory of the *Panzerwaffe* cannot be attributed to the quantitative and qualitative superiority of its tanks, but to the superb leadership of its commanders, the high morale of its crews, the excellent trai-

Two *Panzer IV Ausf As* in the Polish campaign. The highly conspicuous white crosses in the turret were soon abandoned, as they helped the enemy sighting extraordinarily.
Bundesarchiv 101I-012-0016:

ning and the better tactics employed. Other aspects that are often completely forgotten, such as the comparatively excellent optics and the good radio equipment of the German tanks, also played a role in the victory.

Contrary to what happened in Poland, they did have to face considerable enemy armoured forces in the West. And because of that, the limitations of the *Panzer* III in the tank-to-tank combat were clearly unveiled, which would be the decisive factor to make the *Panzer* IV, originally conceived as a support vehicle, to progressively become the main tank. For the *Panzer* IV the Western campaign meant serious losses. By late May 1940,

Only a handful of Panzer IVs took part in the Polish campaign, like this one of the Ausf B version.

A *Panzer IV Ausf C* overtakes a column of Greek and British prisoners in the flashing push across Greece.

Bundesarchiv 101I-063-0332

sixty-three of the 290 that had started the campaign were total losses, a very high loss percentage. This can be compared, for instance, with what was going on in the same date with the *Panzer* II, 150 of which had been lost out of a total inventory of 1,092. The high *Panzer* IV losses were obviously due to the fact that, instead of being used in the escort vehicle mission for which they were initially conceived they had to launch into the heat of combat.

However, inertia was going to play a bad trick on the Germans. The limitations of the *Panzer* III were becoming evident. The need to produce more *Panzer* IVs and improve its performances in armour and artillery did not cease, but after all, the success in the West against very superior enemy armoured forces was so smashing that it had a drowsy effect. In other words, it did not seem necessary to introduce great nor radical improvements in future campaigns in which the likeliest ene-

The *Panzer IV* had a crew of five, all of whom carried out their tasks in claustrophobic conditions. Their black uniforms were thought to conceal the spots, but soon became the symbol of an elite corps.

Bundesarchiv 101I-063-0332

mies were not supposed to have better equipment than that used by France and Britain. However, in the event of the planned amphibious operation against Britain, forty-two *Panzer* IVs (and 168 *Panzer* IIIs), were converted

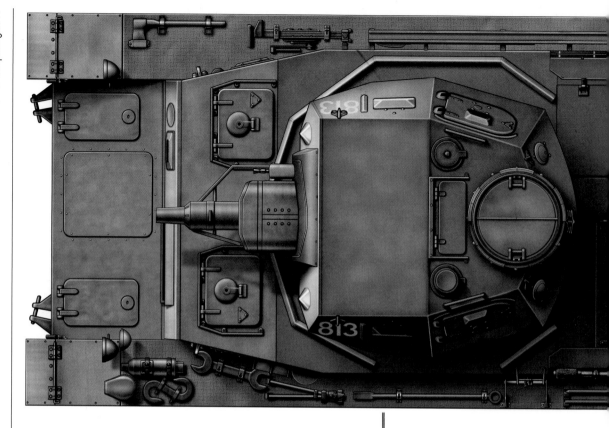

Previous page: when the last elements of the *Afrika Korps* surrendered in Tunis on the 13 May 1943, which was also the end of the *21.Panzer Division*. On 6 July that same year, the *schnelle Division West* –quartered in France– was renamed the *21.Panzer-Division West neu*. The first battalion of its tank regiment –the *Panzerregiment 100*– was equipped with *Pz.Kpfw* Vs, whereas the second one was a mixture of short-barrelled *Panzer* IV *Ausf B/Cs*, *Panzer* IV *Ausf Hs*, and French Hotchkiss *Pz.Kpfw* 35 H 734(f)s and Somua *Pz.Kpfw* 35 S 739(f)s *Beutepanzer*.

May 1944, the *Panzerregiment 22* –the new designation of the *Panzerregiment 100*– carrying out exercises near the village of Saint-Martin-de-Fresnay. A *Panzer Ausf C* of the *8.Kp* stops at Madame Leroy's café and the crew gets off for a snack.

The tank is a veteran of previous campaigns, judging from its condition, numerous dents everywhere, torn-off and not replaced mudguards, etc.

Bundesarchiv 101I-721-0378-28 y 101I-721-0378-33a

The gunners in the turret of a *Panzer* IV. The relative roominess allowed fitting a more powerful gun later.

into *Tauchpanzer* –submersible tanks– by July 1940. The tanks thus modified could operate at a depth of up to 15 metres. They were to be launched from ships with ramps off the shore, which they should reach by "sailing submerged." The invasion was cancelled but, assigned to new units, the *Tauchpanzer* IVs built carried out a spectacular operation, wading submerged across the mighty Bug river in the early days of the Russian campaign.

The *Panzerkampfwagen IV Ausf* Ds and Es were normally fitted with an extra armour plate in the front of the superstructure. The pictures were taken at the Krupp-Grusonwerk factory in Magdeburg.

New OBs were introduced in February 1941. The medium companies, one per battalion, should now have fourteen *Panzer* IVs and five *Panzer* IIs. But the Russian campaign started and the *Panzerwaffe* was far from having the *Panzer* IV tanks necessary for

6

that. As a matter of fact, the tank inventory on 1 June 1941 still included 877 *Panzer* Is (although many of them were assigned to training tasks); Czech tanks were still in very significant numbers, 754 *Panzer* 38(t)s and 170 *Panzer* 35(t)s. 1,074 *Panzer* IIs were still in service; but the highest figures corresponded now to the *Panzer* III, 350 with the short-barrelled 37 mm gun and 1,090 with the 50 mm gun. As regards the *Panzer* IV, they num-

bered 517, including those of the last versions, the *Ausf E* and the *Ausf F*.

The *Ausf E* was the result of an order also placed in January 1938, but it was built from

A *Panzer* IV *Ausf D* of the *5.Panzer-Division* in the French campaign, during which the limitations of the Panzer III in tank-to-tank combat became evident, which gave rise to the growing leading role of the *Panzer* IV.

Bundesarchiv 101I-124-250.

September 1940 to April 1941 and totalled 223. As regards the Ausf F, it was the first version ordered once the war had started, but deliveries did not begin until that April 1941 and continued into March 1942.

Top and bottom: a *Panzer* IV *Ausf D* on training in Germany in an exercise in mount and wood areas, similar to the Ardennes, through which the attack on the West was launched. It belonged to the *Panzer-Regiment* 1

Bundesarchiv 146-1981-070-15 y 16

May and June 1940, the Panzertruppen obtained their greatest success on superior enemy armoured forces.
Bundesarchiv 101-055-1599-31

This is the most typical image of the Panzer IV in the Western campaign.
Bundesarchiv 101-124-0211-18

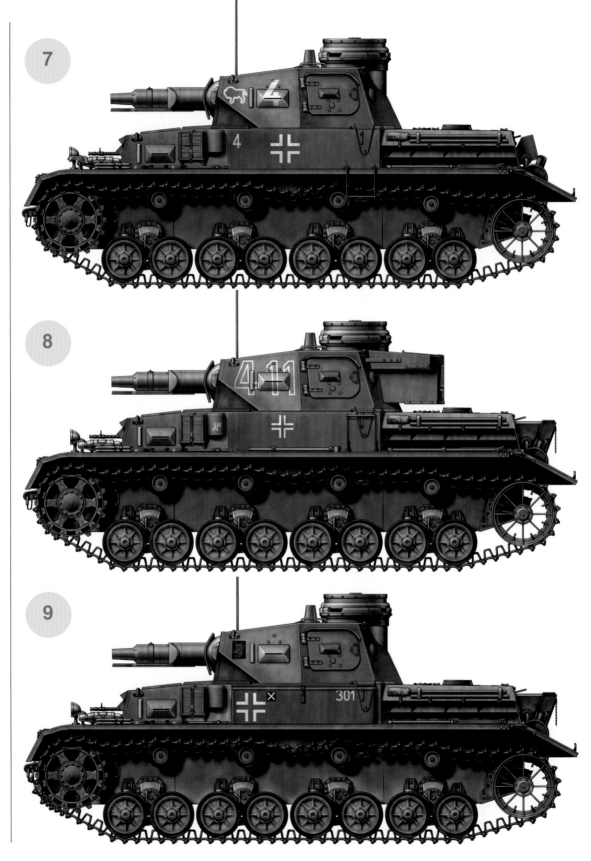

Previous page: France 1940. The whole crew of this *Panzer* IV is posing happy and radiant, the very image of victory.

Top: not propaganda now, several *Panzer* IV (of the *Ausf* D and E version) in a yard used by maintenance crews.

Bundesarchiv 1101I-063-2162-30a y 101I-0924-216-11

A *Panzer* IV towed onto a trailer on the Russian front, October 1941. Notice the welded track fragments on the side of the hull: an interim solution to reinforce the weak armour.

Bundesarchiv 146-1994-011-23

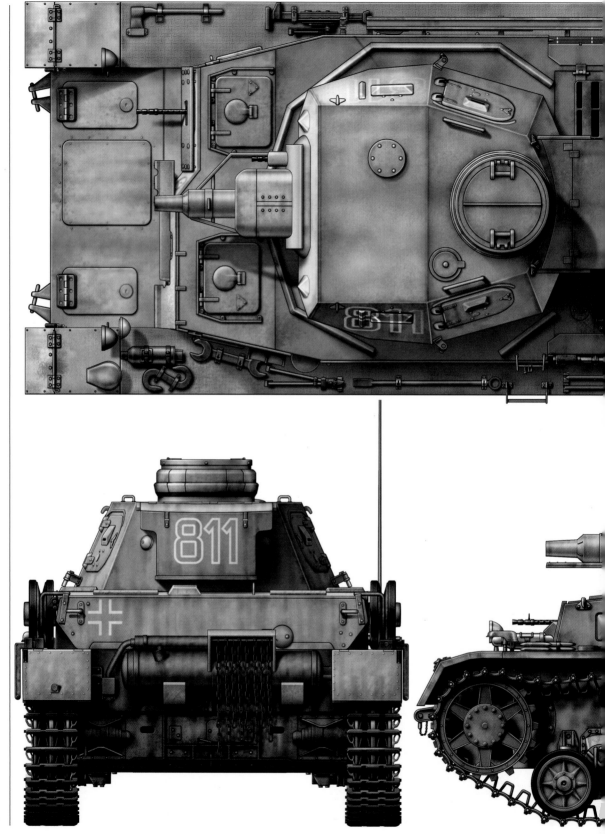

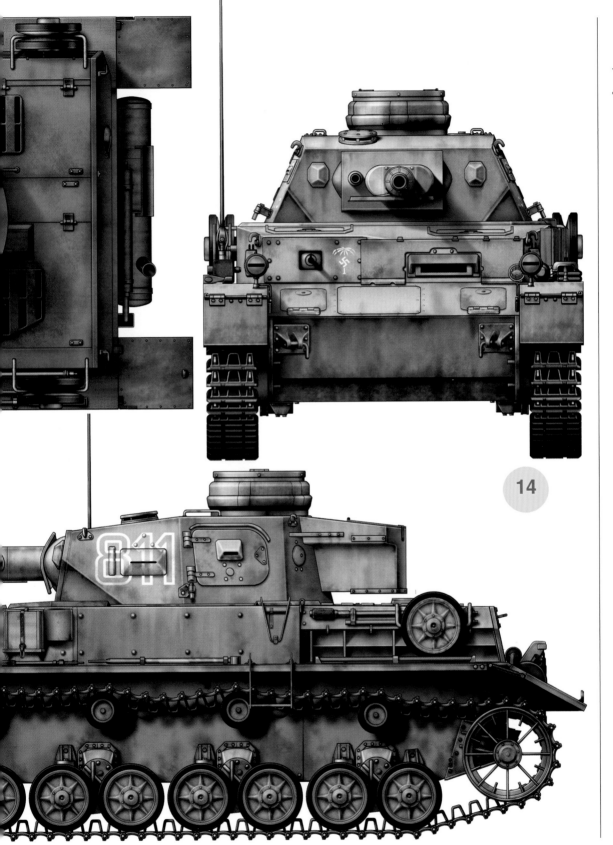

14

A *Panzer* IV *Ausf E* of the *11.Panzer Division* in Yugoslavia. The additional armour, bolted to the hull, is conspicuous.
Bundesarchiv 101I-770-0280-20

Next page. A very delicate moment: this *Panzer* IV has to be helped out, as it almost fell off a bridge that has given way beneath.
Bundesarchiv 146-1975-078-21a y 146-1994-009-33

On the *Ausf* E version, armour thickness increased to 50 mm for the first time, but only in the front of the hull. But additional armoured plates of 30 and 20 mm of thickness respectively were bolted to the front and side of the superstructure. Quite an improvised solution, but it was the only viable at the moment to correct the obvious weakness of the armour. Other modifications affected the commander's cupola, the turret design, etc. A total of 223 entered service, vanishing from the German armour inventory in 1944.

The *Ausf* F version was a real climax. In the first place, the initial order for 625 was a big one, to be built by Krupp and Vomag and Nibelungswerke as well. Armour in the entire front reached 50 mm, and 30 mm in all of the side-walls, giving up bolted plates. The weight of the tank now, of course, was much heavier, growing from the 18.4 t of the A version to the 22.3 t of that version. Pressure on the ground was already excessive, so it was necessary to increase the width of the track to 40 cm (which also brought changes in the running gear).

Spring 1942. Thaw has come and mud becomes a new enemy for this *Panzer* IV.
Bundesarchiv 101I-269-0211-10

15

Two views of *Panzer* IV *Ausf Gs* in Russia, summer 1941. Top, the crew watch the difficult advance of the Panzer IIs. Bottom, the advance on Leningrad.

Fotos: Bundesarchiv 101-265-0040a-22 y 101-351-1427-21a

The off-road virtues of a tank are evident in this photo.
Bundesarchiv

Although the tanks available to the *Panzerwaffe* at the start of the Russian campaign were noticeably better than at the first campaign –that of Poland, the combat power of each *panzer* division was not much greater. And the reason is that orders had been issued to double the number of *panzer* divisions, but this had been achieved by the expeditious method of leaving each division with one single *panzer* regiment, instead of the two that had started the war. The division's infantry, on the other hand, had incre-

Distances in Russia were themselves a very serious problem for the *panzers*.

Bundesarchiv

ased from one to two regiments. But obviously, an infantry regiment does not have the firepower of an armoured one. Besides, for the first time, the Germans were forced to move part of their combat force to secondary fronts. For that reason, out of more than 500 *Panzer* IVs extant in June 1941, only 438 of them (of the B to the F versions) took part in the launching of Operation «Barbarossa», as the rest were in training units or elsewhere, operating with Rommel in Africa.

The Russian campaign was a tremendous challenge for the *Panzerwaffe* from the start. From the beginning, the Red Army was a tough enemy, who did not admit defeat and fought energetically, which caused the German losses to mount, including also –of course– those of tanks. Distances were huge and tanks had to run nearly always on their own, as there were no suitable roads, no trailers or railway lines. Weather conditions were terrible at all seasons (too hot in summer and terribly cold in winter, extremely rainy in spring and autumn, which made dirt into mud). All of this took a tremendous brunt on tanks. It is difficult to knock out a tank for good, for which reason the figures of *panzers* deployed in Russia on paper, always supposed relatively high amounts. No matter how

16

17

18

A factory-fresh *Panzer* IV *Ausf F1*. It was the last version armed with a short gun. From an "escort tank", it became a "main battle tank".
Bundesarchiv 146-1979Anh-001-10

sophisticated a war machine it is, at the same time it is very fragile, with so many factors against, a great number were unserviceable for long periods, necessary for maintenance tasks, battle damage repairs, etc. For this reason, rather than the amounts of tanks deployed in Russia, only the operational figures at a moment were significant, and here figures were alarmingly low.

On the other hand, the Soviet Armoured Arm was also a formidable enemy from the start. At the beginning, it was a matter of numbers; the Soviets seemed to have an

endless amount of tanks (about 20,000 at the start of the campaign). But soon an even more terrible factor emerged, qualitative superiority. Never in its whole history did the *Panzerwaffe* suffer a blow comparable to the discovery of the Russian T-34s and KVs. The event has a recorded date, 3 July 1941, west of Smolensk, when the 3 *Panzergruppe* was the subject of a mass attack by 600 Soviet tanks including, for the first time, the T-34. That event shook up the self-confidence of the German tank crews for good.

Panzer IV losses in the six first months of the campaign in Russia were appalling. From the 21 June, when the campaign started, to the 31 December, 348 of them became total losses (other sources mention 369), whereas many others were so damaged or so worn out that they were not operational for long periods. It should be reminded that the campaign was started with 438. On the other

This close-up of a *Panzer* IV *Ausf F1* shows the *5.Panzer Division* badge –an X on a black background– and its 31 *Panzer Regiment*, a devil's head.
Bundesarchiv 146-1979Anh-001-10

The *«Großdeutschland»* was the first division to have a battalion fully equipped with *Panzer* IVs.

Bundesarchiv: 101-748-0099a-36

A purely propaganda picture, these *Panzer* IV *Ausf F1s* (*Panzer Regiment 31, 5.Panzerdivision*) are posing for the press. The building behind them housed the editorial office of the *Panzerfaust*, one of the newspapers published by the German Propaganda Companies (PK).

Bundesarchiv: 101I-271-0301-30a

The first winter Russian caught the *panzer* crews by surprise, and it took them too long to get used to such a hostile environment.

Bundesarchiv: 101L-215-0354-14

hand, although 330 new ones were delivered by the factories from June to December 1941, the logistic chaos that ruled the early months of «Barbarossa» and the need to attend to the African front as well meant that not all of them could reach the exhausted *panzer* troops fighting in Russia. By December 1941, the situation was so critical that many *panzer* divisions had hardly any equipment to make up an operational *panzer* company. The Germans felt that the *panzer*, the sword of their army, was a dented broken tool.

The German plan makers had already decided to fit a 75-mm long-barrelled gun to what was to be the G version of the *Panzer* IV. But they were in such a hurry that the change was introduced as the production was of the F version went along, thus giving birth to the version known as the *Ausf* F2. By then, 462 tanks of the F version had already been delivered, but the last twenty-five were retained at the factories to modify them as F2s. As regards the F2 version itself, it was built from March to July 1942 and apart from the twenty-five "converted" mentioned above, there were another 175 more.

The gun fitted to the F2 version was the KwK 40 L/43, with a high muzzle velocity (800 metres per second), whose piercing shells were able to beat (without a need to come to tank-to-tank fight as it was going on) any Soviet, British or American tank in service at the time at reasonable combat distances. Fortunately, the size of the turret and the hull of the *Panzer* IV allowed housing the new gun and bulkier ammunition. What is more, if all the versions had been able to carry 80 rounds for the gun until then, the *Panzer* IV *Ausf* F2 increased its ammunition capacity up to 87 rounds. The same stock

North Africa, 1941. The hits on the turret of this *Panzer* IV, and even on the gun muzzle, evidence the harshness of combat.

Bundesarchiv: 101L-783-0117-113

was maintained (including high-explosive, piercing, hollow-charge and smoke rounds) in the later versions. When fighting units started to take deliveries of the F2, although in dribs and drabs, hopes were renewed.

In order to prepare the operations to be launched in the southern sector of the Eastern Front in the summer of 1942, the *panzer* divisions taking part were reinforced at the expense of those deployed in other sectors, which were literally reduced to a nominal role. And for the first time an armoured battalion was established made up only of medium companies armed with the *Panzer* IV. Curiously, this battalion was not part of any *panzer* named division, but a Guards' Division of the German Army, the «*Großdeutsch-*

land» Division. But the power of this first medium battalion should not be exaggerated either, as its three companies only numbered ten *Panzer* IVs each, with some more in the staff company. Thus, although the *Wehrmacht* total inventory of *Panzer* IVs was 681 when the great operations started in the southern sector in June 1942, the armoured units taking part in the offensive had just 208 short-barrelled tanks (of the B to the F versions) and another 170 long-barrelled tanks (F2 and G versions). On average, each *panzer* division participating in the 1942 offensive had twelve long-barrelled *Panzer* IVs, the only ones considered to be able to beat the T-34 and the KV. Obviously, that was very little. As a matter of fact, in 1942 the main advantages of the *panzers* over their

A small number of German tanks, like this *Panzer* IV *Ausf F1*, were sent to Norway to prevent an enemy landing.
Bundesarchiv: 101I-113-0029-13

Soviet counterparts were still their excellent gun sights and the better and more complete radio equipment (still a rarity on Soviet tanks), which afforded a much more efficient tactical control. Although the Soviet command had improved its leadership capacity

and crew training, the Germans were still superior in both fields. But the truth is, one should not forget, the Soviet tanks still outperformed the German ones in armour, artillery, off-road capacity and range. The Ausf G was built from May 1942 to June 1943, with a total of 1,687. Until March 1943, they were armed with the same gun as the Ausf F2 version (1,275), but from then onward they were fitted with the even more powerful 75-mm KwK 40 L/48 gun. Armour was the same thickness as in the F2, 50 mm in the front and 30 mm in the sides. When production of this version was at its climax, it was decided to reinforce armour with additional 30-mm plates in the front of the hull and the superstructure, welded in some cases and bolted in others. With that, 770 *Ausf Gs* got additional protection. Protection was still seen as insufficient by the crews, who reinforced the parts most vulnerable to enemy fire by adding spare track parts. But the battlefield was becoming more and more lethal and hollow-charge

The long-barrelled *Panzer* IVs had their baptism of fire on the Russian front in the summer campaign of 1942. A column is depicted; the advance does not stop thanks to the efficient job of the German pontoniers.

The arrival of the long-barrelled *Panzer* IVs allowed the Germans to regain the qualitative superiority on the Eastern front for some time and thus the thrill of carrying out great offensives again.

Bundesarchiv.

The image may look bucolic, but it depicts the terrifying Eastern front. These *Panzer* IV *Ausf F2s* belong to the mythical *«Großdeutschland»* division.

Bundesarchiv 101I-748-0097-23.

Three views of the *Panzer* IV of another famous unit, the *SS-«Leibstandarte Adolf Hitler» Panzer Division*, in the battle for Kharkov. The one in the top has been hit and has lost its tracks.

Bundesarchiv: 101I-330-3021-21a

explosives were particularly effective, even against reinforced armour. In order to face this threat, from March 1943 onwards, the G version was the first to be fitted with the so-called *Schürzen* (aprons, literally), sort of skirt armour, steel plates which hang over the sides of the superstructure and also –in this case, with an appropriately rounded form– of the turret.

As a whole, the year 1942 was less dramatic for the *Panzer* IV. On the Eastern front, 502 *Panzer* IV tanks were lost, i.e. total losses were greater than those of 1941 but we should remind that this refers to a whole year, whereas in the case of 1941 it was only the summer and the autumn. During the month in 1942 with greatest losses recorded (November), 57 were struck off charge, very far, for instance, from the 111 of July 1941. Thus by year's end, the total inventory of *Panzer* IVs first numbered more than 1,000, as monthly production of these tanks had been growing uninterruptedly along the year. It was precisely by December 1942, and for the first time, that factories delivered over 100 a month, 155 exactly.

However, since November that same year, the strategic situation would change dramatically for Germany. The catastrophes occurred between the Volga and the Don, along with the defeat at El Alamein and the Anglo-

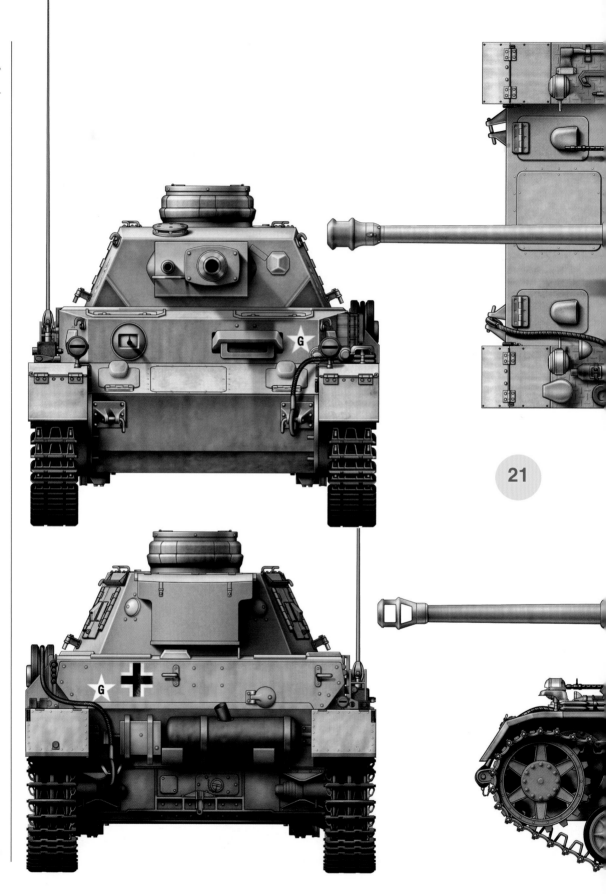

21

American landings in North Africa, was a bad omen for which the *Panzerwaffe* should prepare. And the *Panzer* IV seemed to be the only in a position to face this less and less favourable strategic scene. The *Panzer* VI

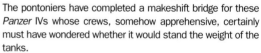
The pontoniers have completed a makeshift bridge for these *Panzer* IVs whose crews, somehow apprehensive, certainly must have wondered whether it would stand the weight of the tanks.

Bundesarchiv

Tigers started to roll off the factories in December 1942, but only in irrelevant amounts. And in their first combat actions, they showed the numerous problems that still plagued them. The *Panzer* V *Panthers* were not available until May 1943, in small numbers as well, and with an incredible series of maintenance problems. On the other hand, production of the *Panzer* III concluded in September 1943. The *Panzer* IV was definitely playing the leading part.

In January 1943, new *panzer* OBs were approved at all levels. In theory, each *panzer* regiment –NB, one per division– should have two medium tank battalions, one of them equipped with *Panzer* IVs and the other with *Panthers*. Besides, each battalion should have a staff company and four companies, instead of the three usual so far. Finally, the strength on paper of each *Panzer*

Top: The armoured grenadiers on top of the *Schützen-panzerwagen* were the comrades of arms of the *panzers*. Bottom: an evidence of the ability of the *Panzer* IV to clear slopes.

Bundesarchiv

The *panzer* units were usually moved from a combat sector to another by rail, as the Germans lacked transport units with trailers. Notice the smoke-grenade launchers on the turret.

Bundesarchiv: 101I-175-1264-06

IV company was established at twenty-two. The purpose, in definitive, was to strengthen the Panzerwaffe as much as possible, which besides would have independent heavy battalions equipped with *Tigers*. But all these changes were, to a great extent, just on paper. They represented an ideal; they did not depict the reality. Many divisions, for instance, were still mostly armed with *Panzer* IIIs. Along the year, and given the teething troubles of the Panther, many regiments were equipped with two *Panzer* IV battalions, and not a single *Panzer* V. What is more, in many armoured battalions that should have been equipped with *Panzer* IVs, the tanks issued were *Sturmgeschütze* (assault guns) instead of *panzers* properly.

The year 1943 saw the birth of the best-achieved variant of the *Panzer* IV, the H version. Deliveries started in April that year and they kept on rolling off the factories until July 1944. In total, 3,774 were built. Front

Also on the remote island of Crete there were some *Panzer* IVs to push back any attack on this strategic Greek island.

Bundesarchiv: 101I-175-1264-06

43

armour finally thickened to 80 mm in the hull and the superstructure, although it remained at 50 mm in the turret and side armour at 30 mm. But in this case, it must be stressed that the hanging Schürzen, with a thickness of 5 mm, provided additional protection. With series production in full swing, it was also decided to make the tanks leave the factory with Zimmerit coating, to counter magnetic anti-tank arms. All these modifications were perceptible externally. But there was also a very remarkable inside, such as a new trans-

This is obviously a training exercise, as the guns of these *Panzer* IV *Ausf Gs* are still protected with their covers. The picture was taken in the Balkans in 1942.
Bundesarchiv: 101I-175-1266-05a

mission, the SSG 77. The weight of the tank finally increased to 25 tons, so speed sank a little inevitably. A more worrying problem was the size and length of the gun, which made the front too heavy, putting too much pressure on the front of the suspension that made the tank pitch. It had been first noticed in the F2, but with the grown-up weight of the H version, it became a serious problem. An unsuccessful attempt was made at modifying the suspension but it remained the same until the end of the war, although it now had to stand a noticeably heavier hull, superstructure and armament.

If the *Panzer* IV is the *panzer* par excellence, the H version is in its turn the one that best represents this tank as, not in vain, it was built in the largest numbers and best synthesized the virtues (and handicaps) of this tank.

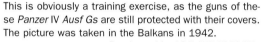

Another picture of the same exercise. The driver drives the tank into a lake under the close watch of other crews.

Bundesarchiv: 101I-175-1267-34

44

Two views of the *Panzer* IVs on the Italian front in 1943. They belong to the *16.Panzer Division* as the badge in the rear of the hull shows.

Bundesarchiv: 101I-305-0652-13 y 17

Since 1943 the *Wehrmacht* was on the defensive. But the *panzers* remained indispensable, urgently coming to any sector under threat.

Colección Javier del Campo

Under the close watch of the crews, these *Panzer* IV *Ausf Gs* carry out a recovery exercise of a tank bogged in the mud.

Bunderarchiv: 101I-175-1268-20a

The turret of this *Panzer* IV *Ausf G* sports the badge of the *Panzer Regiment 4* (*13.Panzer Division*).

But no matter how much improved the H version was as compared to its forerunners, the new reality on the battlefields was totally adverse. On the preparation of the most ambitious operation launched by the Germans that year, Operation *«Zitadelle»*, they placed great hopes in tanks like the *Panther*, the *Tiger* and the *Elefant*. When it came down to it, these types suffered greater losses to mechanic breakdown than to enemy fire, so a huge number of them did not even go into combat. For this reason, as a matter of fact, the main effort eventually fell on the 841 long-barrelled *Panzer* IVs that the Germans concentrated in the *panzer* units of the two arms of the pincer movement that should converge on Kursk. However, everybody knows the result of the battle. In spite of the fact that the Germans now had tanks in amounts never heard of before and of much improved quality, the enemy, specially the Soviets, had such a mass of tanks that it was impossible to beat them. Along 1943, a total of 2,352 *Panzer* IVs became total losses on the Eastern Front, as the combats to stop the Soviet wave did not cease for a moment since the defeat in Kursk.

The year 1944 brought no good omens, as it was obvious that the Western Allies would try to land in northwest Europe, a real cause of concern for the Germans, much more than the incredibly slow progression of their armies along the Italian Peninsula. For the first time, an important armoured mass had to be deployed in France. Rather than permanent garrisons, they were actually units coming from the Eastern Front for rest, reorganization and re-equipment. But the

At the bottom of the Acropolis in Athens, these *Panzer* IVs on parade are basically playing a propaganda role: to convince the enemy of the presence of important armoured forces in that sector, which was actually almost devoid of armoured troops.

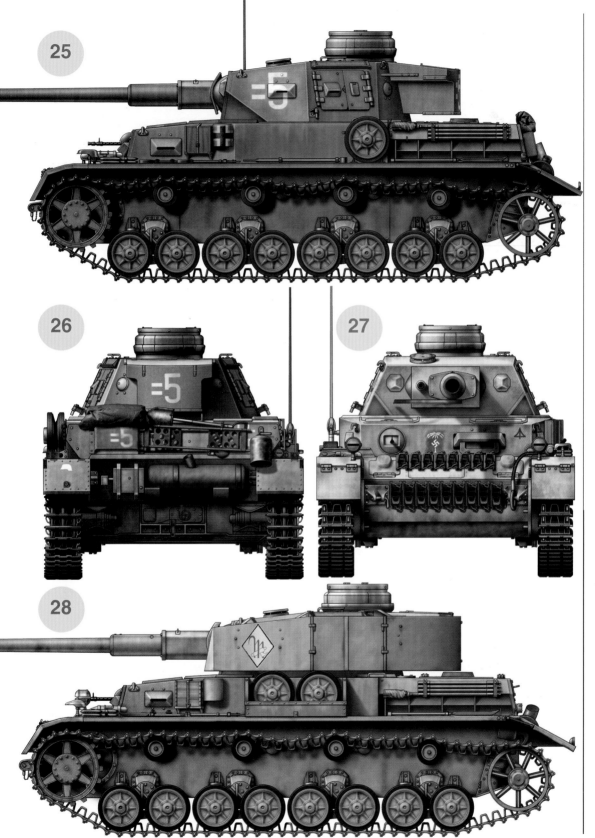

truth is that an important part of the German armoured inventory was rolling on the French countryside. When the Western Allies set a foot on France, nearly 750 *Panzer* IVs, for instance, were there and most of them were of the most modern version then, the H, for –as we pointed out above– these were units that were in the process of rearmament. Given the way in which the invasion campaign developed, a large part of these tanks were lost. But again, it was in the East that losses were more catastrophic. All along 1944, in a succession of memorable coups, the Red Army was defeating one after another each German army group they met. Some of them, like the German Centre and the South Ukrainian Army Groups were literally annihilated. Once and again, the *panzers* were launched into the counterattack to stop the breakthroughs or to cause a local defeat to the most adventured enemy vanguards. The *Panzer* IV was the real workhorse in these operations. But, in definitive, no significant victory was achieved. In

Previous page. Although fitted with skirt armour on the hull and the turret, the crew of this *Panzer* IV must have thought it was not enough so they have reinforced the front of the hull with links and the upper part of the turret with a steel plate.
Bundesarchiv: 101I-694-0308a-28a

Summer 1943, central Russia. Although by that time of the war the *Tiger* and the *Panther* were already available, the well-proven *Panzer* IV (in this case of the *Ausf G* version), still remained the backbone of the *Panzertruppen*.
Bundesarchiv: 101I-687-0127-18

1944, 2,643 *Panzer* IVs were total losses on the Eastern Front. Losses were more and more difficult to make up, so in the last months, new OBs were established for the companies equipped with *Panzer* IVs, which saw their number finally reduced to ten each.

The *Waffen SS* units eventually became an important percentage of the *Panzertruppen*. In the picture, tank crews of the *12.SS-Panzer Division «Hitlerjugend»*.
Bundesarchiv: 101I-297-1725-09

This is the typical picture of the *Panzer* IV of the *Ausf H* version, of the *Panzer Regiment 29* (*12.Panzer Division*): the *zimmerit* non-magnetic coating covers the hull, and the skirt armour protects the sides and the turret.

Bundesarchiv: 101I-088-3734a-19

One more *Panzer* IV A*usf H*, in this case of the *2.Panzer Division*, on training exercises in France.

Bundesarchiv: 101I-298-1759-25

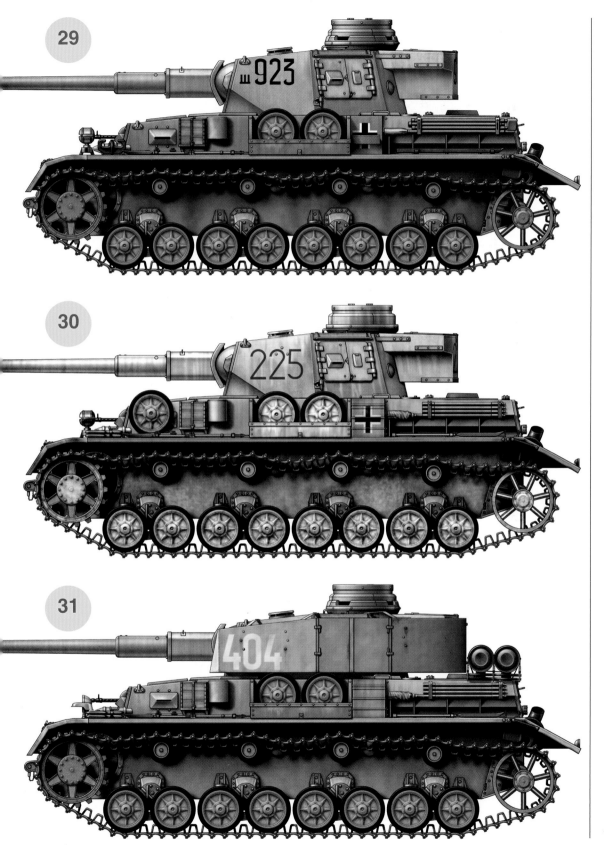

29

30

31

The environment of northern Russia, where the endless birch forests disappear only to be followed by lakes and marshes, was not the most suitable for the use of armoured forces.

Bundesarchiv 101I-700-0273-11

Germany was conscious that she was under siege. Her resources were diminishing, whereas those of the enemy grew exponentially. It was in this context that the last version of the *Panzer* IV was born, the Ausf J. Production started in June 1944 and continued practically to the end of the war, with 1,758 delivered. Now the only maker was the Nibelungswerke company, as Krupp and Vomag were busy with other projects.

This time it was not an improvement but an adaptation forced by the bad times. The most remarkable modification was the elimination of the auxiliary electric motor that powered the turret, and the room now available was filled with an auxiliary tank. As *panzers* literally had to play the firemen, hurrying to each front sector under threat, it was vital

While the pontoniers are still at work, this Panzer IV Ausf H is already moving on it in perfect combat order, driving to the frontline.

Bundesarchiv 101I-689-0194-16a

Top and middle. If the first winter caught the *Panzertruppen* by surprise, that was not the case in the next winters on the Eastern front and the German tank crews were able to maintain a high operational degree.

Bundesarchiv 101/160/153731

to increase their range, and the auxiliary tank brought it to 320 km. A significant detail of the need for the Germans to save raw equipments is that in this version the idler wheels were not four but three. Another very remarkable detail was that in many cases the vehicles of this J version were fitted with side *Schürzen* made of steel mesh, instead of plates. They achieved the same effect against hollow-charge arms and were cheaper and lighter.

Also in 1944 there were another two remarkable versions. So far, command tanks and tanks for forward artillery observers had been based on other types, especially the *Panzer* III. But as production of the latter ceased in 1943, it was necessary to convert a total of 97 *Panzer* IVs for the task between March and September 1944. Thus was born the *Panzerbefehlswagen* IV (although the offi-

An officially forbidden but very common practice, giving the grenadiers a ride on the tank. In this case, it is a *Panzer* IV of the Panzer Regiment 6 (*3.Panzer Division*), as the badge on the skirt armour of the turret reveals.

Bundesarchiv 101I-090-3914-29a.

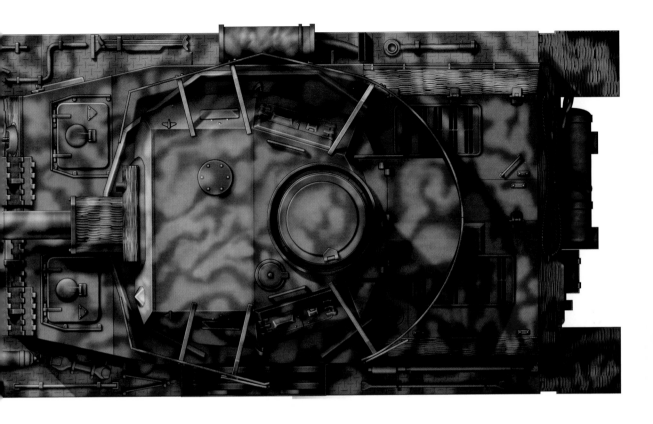

Smooth paint finish on tanks was rare in the last years of the war, but it still existed, as we can see in the case of this picture taken in Ukraine in September 1943.
Bundesarchiv: 101I-240-2142-21

cial name was much longer: *Panzerbefehls-wagen* mit 7,5 KwK L/48). Unlike other previous command tanks, which had no heavy armament, in this case the gun was not removed and replaced with a fake one. The main difference between the command tank and the rest was in the radio equipment, as, besides the usual 10-watt FuG 5 receiver / transmitter fitted to all the *panzers*, from the *Panzer* III to the *Panzer* VI, they were also equipped with the 20-watt FuG 7 or the 30-watt FuG 8.

As regards the modification carried out to house the forward artillery observers, the result was the *Panzerbeobachtungswagen* IV, 90 *Panzer* IVs were reconverted between July 1944 and March 1945. In this case, the radio was a FuG 4, specifically developed for artillery observers, and one of the mentioned FuG 8s. Both the command and the observation tanks were equipped with a periscope.

Previous page. Two views of the *Panzer* IV *Ausf H*. Top, a crew has now gained great ability to use track links to reinforce the armour. Bottom, the ever-tiring maintenance tasks.
Bundesarchiv 101I/155/2142/32

Finally, it must be noticed that another thirty-six *Panzer* IVs had been converted into recovery tanks (*Bergepanzer* IV) as well, between October and December 1944, by suppressing the turret and fitting a box-shaped superstructure and a crane.

By 1945, German statistics on tanks, so reliable until then, either became less accu-

A most common damage, the loss of a track. The ground crew has come in aid of this tank crew, who are facing hard work.
Bundesarchiv 101I/155/2142/32

On Belgian soil, a *Panzer* of the *«Hitlerjugend»* Division riding under the close scrutiny of the umpires on an exercise (identified by the white bands on their service-dress caps).

Bundesarchiv 101I-297-1722-23

Another picture of the same division. The engine hatches wide open suggest there is a problem.

Bundesarchiv 101I493-3355-23

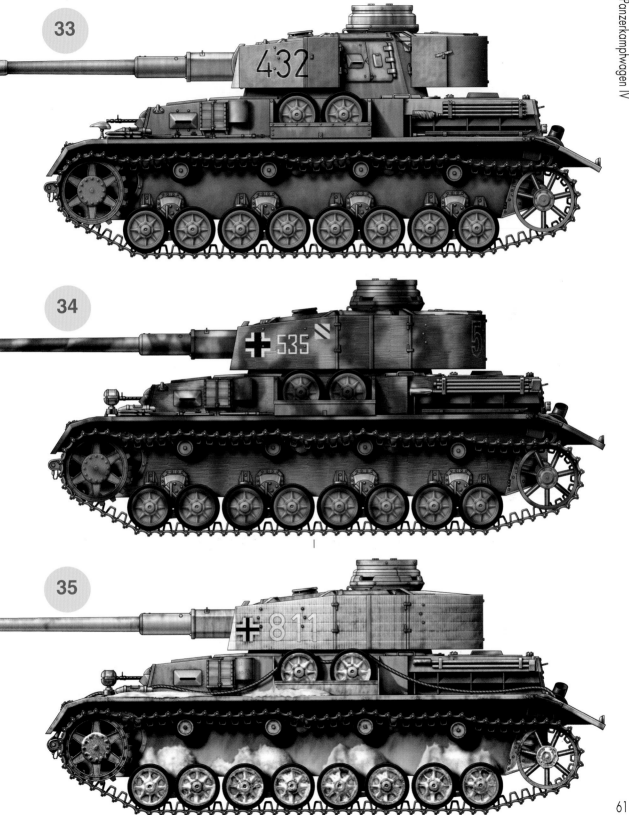

33

34

35

The teenage soldiers of the *12.SS Panzer Division «Hitlerjugend»* used to paint the names of their beloveds on different parts of the tank.

Bundesarchiv: 101I-297-1722-27

Russia, summer 1944. German soldiers pose in front of this *Panzer* IV, which has just got several hits on the turret. Notice that the ground crew have removed the screws of the protector joint of the barrel mounting to disassemble it.

Foto: Bundesarchiv: 101I-297-1722-24

rate or simply vanished. The last month when the total losses of *Panzer* IV are still recorded is January 1945, with 287 on the Eastern Front. By counting them and ignoring the data of February to May that year, at least 6,153 *Panzer* IV tanks were lost fighting the Soviets, a figure that certainly must have been greater actually, as losses for the other months, February to May, were very high. Summing up, approximately 75 % of the *Panzer* IVs were lost to Soviet action. Some more statistics for those who still believe it was the Western Allies who defeated the Germans.

A March 1945 report stated that by that date 793 *Panzer* IVs were still deployed, 603 of them in the East, 59 in the West and 131 in Italy. The same report mentions a total of

This *Panzer* IV of the *«Hitlerjugend»* has no been in combat yet, but the hard training exercises have been enough to damage the mudguards and alter the layout of the side skirt armour.

Bundesarchiv: 101I-297-1722-24

Central Russia, summer 1944. This *Panzer* IV *Ausf J* moves carefully to its firing position.
Foto: Bundesarchiv: 101I-695-0406-03

954 *Panzer* V *Panthers* and 276 *Panzer* VI *Tigers* deployed on the different fronts. So, as we can see, the *Panzer* IV remained an element of the greatest importance in the ever-dwindling *Panzerwaffe* till the end.

The *Panzer* IV was also the most widely exported German tank. The Germans, who could hardly supply their own *Panzerwaffe* properly, had to meet the needs of their allies all the same. In general, they tried to do so by delivering war-booty tanks, but finally it was necessary to supply tanks of German production too. In 1942, the Germans delivered small numbers to Romania and Hungary, as both countries were to cover the long German flank on the Don and it was convenient to strengthen their little efficient armoured forces. The Romanians got eleven *Panzer* IVs (and the same number of *Panzer* IIIs), whereas thirty-two *Panzer* IVs (and ten *Panzer* IIIs) were delivered to the Hungarians. In any case, this equipment

was lost in the great catastrophe on the southern front in the last months of 1942 and early 1943, when the 3rd and 4th

One more picture of a *Panzer* IV *Ausf J*. In this case, it was taken on a training exercise in France.
Bundesarchiv: 101I-298-1761-16

The ever delicate moment of crossing a stream, where it was easy to get stuck, is closely watched by the crew de this *Panzer* IV *Ausf J*, in Ukraine.

Bundesarchiv: 101I-695-0406-03

On the Normandy battlefront: *Panzer IV Ausf.H* of *Panzer Regiment 130*, of the famed *Panzer Lehr Division*.

Bundesarchiv: 101I-298-1761-1   6

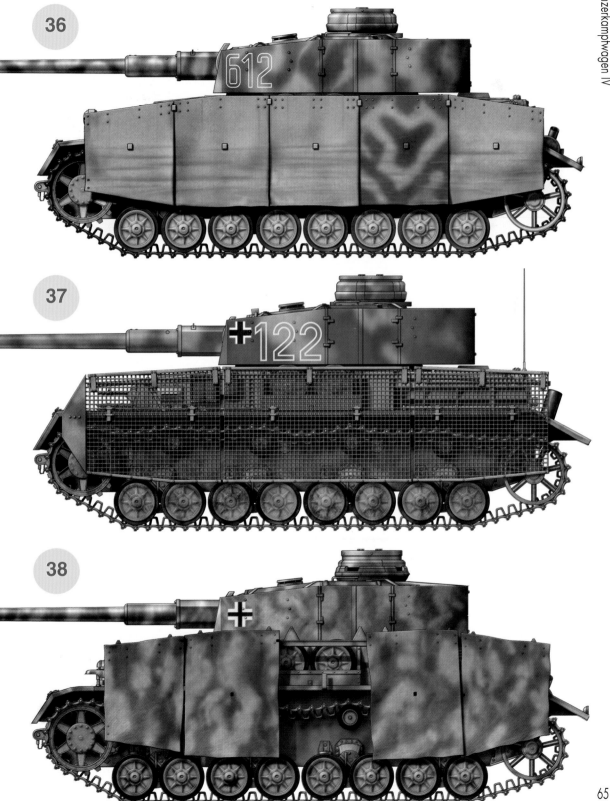

36

37

38

Riding fast towards the enemy. Also in this case the armour of the upper part of the turret has been reinforced with a steel plate.

Bundesarchiv: 101I-689-0190-07

Romanian Armies, and the 2nd Hungarian Army were smashed.

In 1943 the Bulgarians, who also wanted to establish an armoured division, got a new batch. Although Bulgaria did not take part in the fight in the East, the German weakness in southeastern Europe was so great that it seemed useful to reinforce that ally. The Bulgarians thus received forty-six *Panzer* IVs (and ten *Panzer* IIIs). Despite the terrible defeat suffered, Romania kept a high profile on the Russian front, and thus she received *Panzer* IVs in 1943 and until August 1944, a total of thirty-one in 1943 and another 100 along 1944.

Italy found it very difficult to admit the inferiority of her own industry, and thus did not ask the Germans for *Panzer* IVs until very late. In early 1943, it was decided to create an armoured division of the Fascist Militia («Divisione Corazzata CC. NN. 'M'»), which should have an armoured battalion equipped with *Panzer* IIIs, Sturmgeschütz IIIs and *Panzer* IVs, in identical numbers. With that pur-

pose, the Germans delivered twelve *Panzer* IVs. The Italians were still training on them when Mussolini was deposed and the change of regime took place. As the Germans invaded Italy to prevent the defection of their old ally, they recovered the *Panzer* IVs they had delivered.

A small number of *Panzer* IVs (fifteen) were delivered to Finland in 1944 whereas the

In the heat of the combat area in Normandy, a *Panzer* IV *Ausf H* of the *Panzer Regiment* 130, of the prestigious *«Panzer Lehr Division»*.

Bundesarchiv: 101I-277-0835-29

The *zimmerit* non-magnetic coating, generously applied on the hull and also on the skirt armour.

Bundesarchiv: 101I-708-0298-27

other two allies of the Reich, Croatia and Slovakia, got none. In 1944, as the Eastern Front dangerously approached its borders, Hungary decided to ask for the supply of *Panzer* IVs again, and that policy was maintained until 1945, with a total of 62 *Panzer* IVs delivered. In August 1944, both Romania and Bulgaria changed sides and joined the Allies and the *Panzer* IVs supplied by the Germans (in the case of the Romanians, only those surviving, hardly a few dozens), were used against them in the Balkans. Apart from those supplied to the Italians, which returned to German hands, the total of *Panzer* IVs delivered to the Reich allies thus totalled 297, a figure that may seem ridiculous but not so for the amounts the Germans used to deal with. Two countries that were not Axis allies, but whose friendship Berlin was interested in keeping, Turkey and Spain, also received small numbers of *Panzer* IVs.

Once the Second World War was over, the

Russian front, winter 1943-1944. The tasks of the tanks were now mainly defensive and they had to be carried out in close contact with the infantry they had to protect.

Bundesarchiv: 101I-277-0835-29

Ps. 221-5

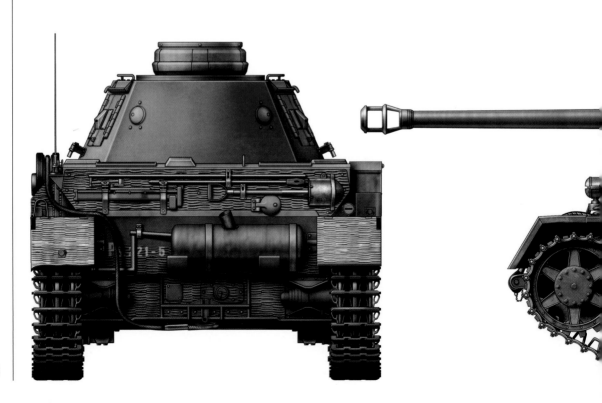

39

Storia Militare

country that made a larger use of the *Panzer* IV was the newly born Czechoslovakia. Before the communists took power in 1948, Czechoslovakia considered the establishment of a powerful armoured force to face the poten-

tial Polish and Hungarian enemies. Some 120 *Panzer* IVs were recovered and, renamed T-40/75N, served in the Czech Army for several years until the latter, now under communist control, was fully equipped with Soviet armament.

A *Panzer* IV of the Turkish Army. A very curious tank, probably the result of frontline workshop modifications, with a hybrid D/E hull broken in the front, without additional armour and a circular machinegun socket. The turret corresponds to an H model and does not have the brackets for the skirt armour. To top it all, the 75-mm gun corresponds to a G model!

Bundesarchiv: 101I-277-0835-29

40

421

41

42

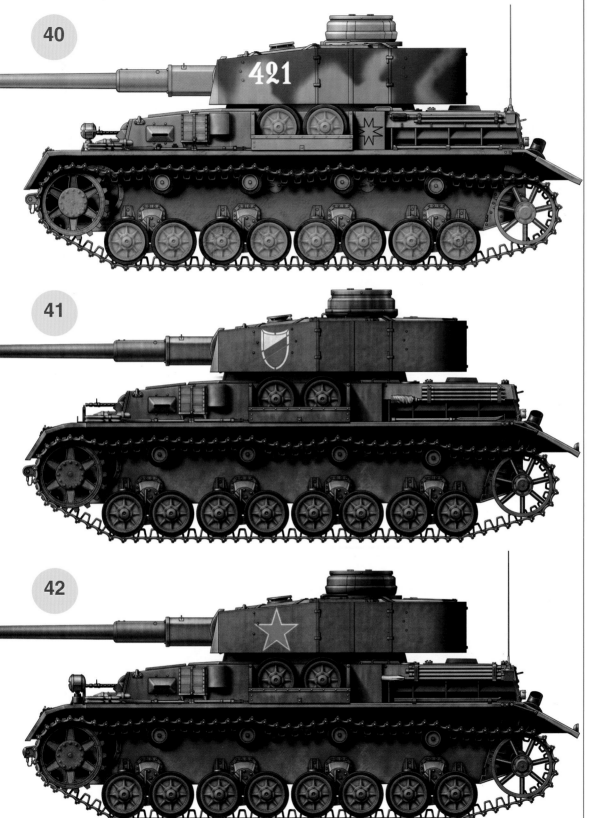

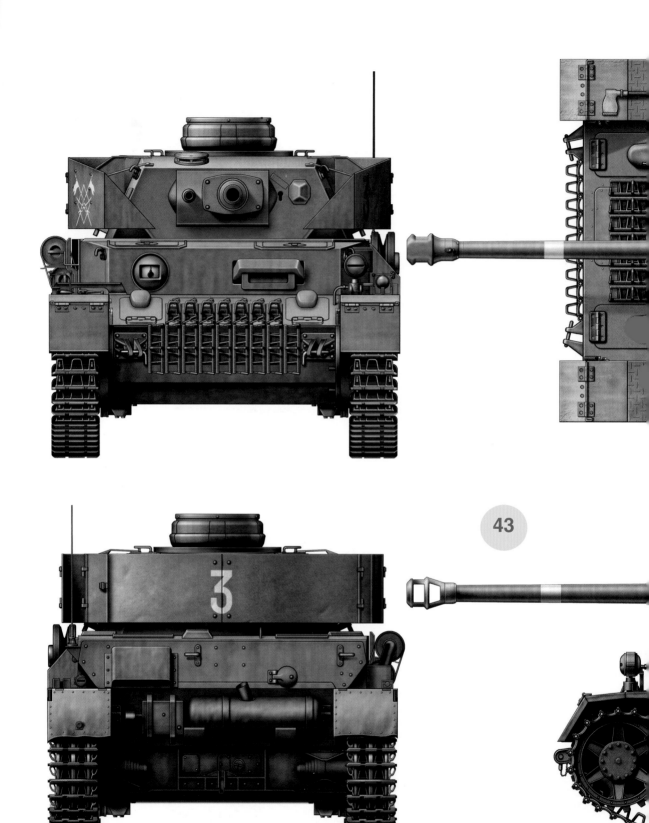

43

CHAPTER II

PANZER IVs FOR THE SPANISH ARMY

Some confusion has often surrounded both the origins and the reasons for the presence of this excellent product of Hitler's war industry in Spain. Some sources, which are even nowadays quoted sometimes on this and other matters, validated with some reservations –to be honest– the following unlikely thesis. It is said that a German merchant vessel of an unrecorded name called at a Spanish port, namely Cartagena, escaping from the Allies with a precious cargo for Erwin Rommel's mythical troops, the *Afrika Korps* –where they were still supposed to be by late 1943! Included in the precious cargo that was interned by the Spanish government with the ship, there were twenty *Panzerkampfwagen IV Ausf H* tanks that were immediately taken over by the *Ejército de Tierra* (Army) that was in bad need to swell its diminished and mauled armoured inventory.

This version, which might be a possible explanation for the presence in Spain of these war machines with some remarks, is not-

hing but fantasy[1]. It is more the result of approaching the confirmation of a proved fact –the physical presence of the tanks– rather than of trying to reconstruct the quite complex history of the commercial relations between Spain and Germany in the hard years of the Second World War.

With a bet on the second option, we shall try to explain the history of the German *Pan-*

Spanish *Panzer* IVs on parade at the *Paseo de la Castellana*, Madrid. For ten years, this was the most modern tank of the *Ejército*.

Via José María Manrique García

zer IV in the Spanish Army in the following pages.

Needs of armoured equipment

After the Civil War, the Spanish armoured inventory was mostly made up of two types of tanks, designated ever since as *Tipo I* and *Tipo II*.

Tipo I were the *Panzerkampfwagen* I and Fiat L3-35 types that had come from Germany and Italy during the conflict, as an aid to the Nationalist side. Both were light tanks, the German one was armed with two 7.92-mm machine guns in a small turning turret and the Italian one had two 7-mm machine guns in a fixed front mount. Both had a crew of two, a tank commander/gunner and a driver.

The so called *Tipo II* was no other than the T-26B tank, sent by the Soviet Union to the republican side and captured in large numbers during the war by the nationalists, who used it profusely. It was a modern combat vehicle, armed with a powerful 45-mm gun and one or two 7.92-mm Degtyarev machine guns (it could even take three).

The *Panzer* IVs were the undisputed protagonists of all the military parades in Madrid. Here, going past the presiding platform on a parade in the capital of Spain in the late forties.

Via José María Manrique García

The then head of the Spanish state, Francisco Franco, presiding over a victory parade in the fifties. In the background, a *Panzer* IV *Ausf H* company of the *Regimiento «Alcázar de Toledo»*.

Via José María Manrique García

Two years and a half after the end of the conflict, the number of tanks still in service in Spain totalled 283, 144 *Tipo I* (*Panzer I Ausf A-B* and Fiat L3-35) and 139 *Tipo II* (T-26B)[2].

Stopping to a halt. The German tanks on the drill ground at San Gregorio, on an exercise with the *Academia General* cadets.

Círculo Trubia, via J. M. Manrique García

In this context, with obsolete worn-out equipment, totally outmoded in the circumstances imposed by the world war and with the additional problem of the chronic lack of spares, some hope seemed to brighten up when Germany, in a bad need of vital stuffs for the running of the war, officially accepted to send armament to make up the negative balance of her trade with Franco's Spain.

Although in a synthesized way, we have already introduced and commented the origins and the meaning of the so-called «Bär» Programme somewhere else[3]. So let's start the story in Berlin on 15 March 1943, at the conference hall of the OKW, where the Spanish Delegation headed by *General de Artillería* Carlos Martínez de Campos was negotiating the acquisition of military equipment for our Army.

Spanish requests, as it has often been said, were always intended to obtain a greater quantity of equipment that exceeded the real needs of the time, as the Spanish negotiators were fully aware that, whatever the case, Germany would actually reduce the amounts delivered.

In this case, the request transmitted by Martínez de Campos to the German Commission was recorded in the document under the heading "Proposal of Equipment and Armament to be acquired. 2nd Group, List no. 11: Armoured Equipment."

That request included 250 tanks with a 45 or a 50-mm gun and two 7.92-mm machine guns[4]; and 100 tanks with a 75-mm gun and two 7.92-mm machine guns[5]. As expected, the German counterproposal only included "a Mixed Group made up of twenty M-IV tanks and 10 *StuG* III assault guns." By making some simple calculations, it can be deduced that the tanks offered did not even reach six percent of those Spain asked for.

One month and a half later, on 29 April, and after a trip to Madrid to explain his superiors the German availability of arms, Martínez de Campos returned to Berlin with the respective list of "items" accepted by Spain, including obviously the Panzer IVs. "That is better than nothing," more than one must have thought under the circumstances.

Training in Germany
In order to train crews in the use of modern tanks, German authorities were asked permission to send a Spanish team to gain the necessary knowledge "on the spot". This request, with a list of the personnel

necessary for training, got a positive answer from the OKW on 19 May. Training was to be carried out at the tank school at Wünsdorf, and this was the personnel required.

Battalion Staff

- 1 Chief
- 1 Adjutant
- 1 Aid (-de-Camp) (*Ordennanz Offizier*)
- 1 Radio Officer
- 1 Chief Radio Operator
- 6 Radio Operators
- 2 Automobile Drivers

Workshop Section

- Officer (Engineers)
- 1 Foreman
- 12 Fitters

Support Group (*Bergegruppe*)

- 3 NCOs
- 1 Armourer NCO
- 2 Assistant Armourers

Each company:

Combat Group
- 5 Officers
- 25 NCOs

Repairs Section
- 3 NCOs
- 10 Men

Train
- 1 Warrant Officer
- 1 Carriage Assistant
- 1 Chief Wireless Operator
- 1 Armourer NCO
- 1 Accountant
- 3 Assistant Armourers

The truth is, such a numerous group was widely reduced once the course in Germany was actually planned. Spanish authorities did not see it convenient to send so many personnel to Germany but just a representation of the two Infantry units this equipment was intended for.

On 5 June 1943, a team made up of twenty-six Spaniards arrived at Wünsdorf, a town very close to the capital of the *Reich*, where the Tank School and the Training Regiment were based, for a training course on the *Parzerkampfwagen* IV.

On 23 June, a communication from the OKW to the Spanish Commission (No. 5744/43) stated that, apart from the supply of the twenty M-IV tanks planned and accepted by Germany, the corresponding body of the *Wehrmacht* had given a green light to a request from Martínez de Campos, regarding the consignment of two additional tanks for the Group Staff. With that purpose, the OKW pointed out to the Spanish that they were about to deliver: "... *two III tanks with 5-cm gun, mod. 42 (Special Vehicle 267)*..." The answer from the Spanish was both sensible and categorical: in order not to diversify the types of tanks in service in Spain even further, it was preferable that the two command tanks be of the type M-IV, identical to the twenty received. And so it was... although in the end, it was useless.

The contracts

The Military Attaché of the Spanish Embassy in Berlin, Mr Carlos Marín de Bernardo, an Engineers colonel, was in charge of negotiating and signing all the contracts with the suppliers of the military equipment of the «*Bär*» Programme. Regarding the tanks, a purchase contract was signed with the Fried Krupp Aktiengesellschaft company of Essen. In that contract, signed in Berlin on 9 December 1943, Article I specified "... *the Spanish Army Ministry agrees with Krupp to the supply of:*

a) *20 IV tanks with 7.5-cm L/48 gun (Kw.K.40) complete with chassis, superstructure, turret and electric wiring, each tank with a mod. 34 machinegun mounted in the turret and another one in the ball armour mount on the*

PANZERKAMPFWAGEN IV Ausf H recibidos en España, dotados de equipo de radio Fu 5											
Vagón nº	8997	9613	20310	5434	20905	3010	12139	15071	20630	5067	12679	3495
Carro nº	84579	84583	84608	84609	84611	84617	84619	84624	84627	84630	84632	84634

PANZERKAMPFWAGEN IV Ausf H recibidos en España, dotados de equipos de radio Fu 5 y Fu 2							
Vagón nº	23020	1193	22624	9992	14364	8153	6264	6606
Carro nº	84587	84606	84614	84622	84623	84629	84631	84633

The then Borbón cadet, the future king Juan Carlos I of Spain, had his picture taken at the driving seat of a *Panzer* IV after the graduation manoeuvres at the *Academia General Militar*, Saragossa.

Círculo Trubia, via J. M. Manrique García

superstructure. All of the twenty will be fitted with an Fu 5 SE 10 U radio set and eight of them will also be fitted with an Fu 2 radio for special purposes.

b) 20 sets of tools and accessories

c) 3 sets of spares

d) 3 sets of spares for engines and transmissions."

Besides, there was also a contract for the following consignments of ammunition:

a) 6,000 Type 39 7.5-cm piercing shell complete rounds

b) 4,000 Type 34 7.5-cm high-explosive shells complete rounds

c) 127,680 Type S.m.K. machine gun cartridges, including 63,840 tracers

d) 20 Z 85 destructor charges for engines and 20 Z 72s for guns.

According to Article IX of the contract, the cost of all the equipment amounted to 7,157,078.45 *Reichmarks*, not including shipment and insurance against "war risks"[6]. Besides, the raw materials required for the production of the equipment to be delivered were also specified, including 8,360 kg of chrome, 540 kg of molybdenum, 1,800 kg of copper, 3,060 kg of brass, 480 kg of red brass, 240 kg of bronze and 2,340 kg of raw rubber.

As an increase on the latter, a second contract was signed in Berlin a few days later, by which Krupp committed themselves to suppl-

ying the Spanish Ministry of the Army with two type IV command tanks, with 7.5-cm L/48 guns (KwK 40), both fitted with an Fu 5 SE 10 U radio for special purposes, an Fu 8 SE 30 radio, a set of accessories for command tanks, two sets of accessories and tools, a set of spares and a set of spares for engines and guns. Apart from the tanks, an ammunition contract was also signed for them, 600 Mod. 39 piercing shells, 400 high-explosive mod. 34 shells, 6,384 7.92-mm Type S.m.K. (half of them tracers) rounds and two destructor charges for engines and another two for guns.

Both constituted Consignment 59 of the *Restprogramm* (2nd phase of the «*Bär*» Programme).

The tanks arrive

Train No 17 of the 2nd phase of the programme, apart from assorted equipment for the Spanish *Marina* (Navy)[7], brought the twenty *Panzer* IV tanks. The total price for the purchase, recorded on Bill No 119-51/150818 of 8 December 1943, was 5,260,000 RM[8], in accordance with the bases for this type of equipment established in the economic talks held in Madrid. The train arrived at the station of Irún on 6

December, the equipment was received by *comandante* Vidaurreta, of the Army General Staff. Once the German wagons were downloaded, the *Agrupación de Movilización y Prácticas de Ferrocarriles* (Railway Training and Mobilization Group) took charge of the panzers, transferred them to Spanish wagons and moved them to Madrid and Seville[9].

But instead of the twenty tanks expected at the station of Irún, only eighteen arrived that 6 December 1943. The cause was that two of the special wagons (FFM type) that carried them encountered mechanical problems and were thus retained in France until they were repaired, to arrive at the border at Irún on the 15th of the same month.

The load on train no 19 included Consignments No 61 and 62 (Bill No 1213-51/150818 of 18-1-44 Krupp):

- 2.400 G.R. mod. 34 at 97 RM........232.800 RM
- 3.600 G.P. mod 39 at 144,5 RM ....520.200 RM
- 63.840 cartridges de 7,92 mm ...10.597,45 RM
- 63.840 tracer cartridges..............14.344,85 RM
- 20 charges, at Z 85 a 20 RM ....400 RM
- 20 charges, at Z 72 a 10,5 RM ....210 RM
TOTAL...**778.552,30 RM**

This equipment was part of the two ammunition supplies for tanks, ordered by the Spanish Commission along with the *Panzer* IV.

Finally, the rest of the ammunition supplies for the tanks, Bill No 1248-51/150817 of 10-3-44, for a total of 502,000 RM was sent on train no 21.

The *Panzer* IVs in Spain

Upon reception, the twenty tanks were assigned to the recently established Armoured Division, based on the German pattern. Half of these new powerful tanks were sent to *Regimiento de Tanques nº 61 «Alcázar de Toledo»*[10], based in Madrid. The other half, to *Regimiento nº 62 «Brunete»*[11], in Seville.

A few days later, there was a stir in military milieus regarding the number of tanks expected from Germany. The number transposition concerning the *Panzer* IVs had originated from some lists going round the ministry milieus, based on the economic talks held in Madrid in July 1943 by the Hispano-German technical sub-commissions. Those lists –probably by mistake– said that the mixed tank group to be sent to Spain was made up of

twenty-four M-IV tanks and six *StuG* III assault guns. However, as we have seen, both the official lists and the contracts mentioned twenty tanks and ten assault guns, apart from the two command tanks. A communication from the Attaché in Berlin to *coronel* Jesús Aguirre, of the Army General Staff, clarified the matter and "righted wrongs"[12].

Each of the two regiments established a company, made up of three three-tank sections and a command tank, using one of the regular tanks for the task, as those expected from Germany would never come.

In 1949, the *Regimiento de Tanques «Brunete» nº 62* was disbanded, the name was assumed by the Armoured Division, and the equipment was allotted to *«Alcázar de Toledo» nº 61* and *«Oviedo» nº 63* Tank Regiments, the latter at Laucién (Morocco), as well as to several cavalry units. The ten *Panzer* IVs of *Regimiento nº 62* were handed over to the *«Alcázar de Toledo»* to establish –with the ten they already had–, the 2nd Armoured Battalion, which coexisted for several years with the obsolete Soviet T-26Bs.

After the supply of American tanks, some of the *Panzer* IVs of the *«Alcázar de Toledo»* were handed over to No 63 Tank Regiment *«Oviedo»* at Laucién[13], which kept them in service until mid-1957, when the regiment was declassified as Armoured to become *Mixto de Infantería y Morteros*. From then onwards, the Spanish panzers were transferred to the Cavalry, which kept them in service in three regiments, *«Dragones de Santiago»* nº 1, *«Dragones de Almansa»* nº 5 and *«Dragones de Farnesio»* nº 12. Eight years later, in 1965, seventeen tanks of this type were sold to the Syrian Army, which used them in the Golan Heights during the Six Day War in June 1967. It was the swansong of an excellent tank, built by the industry of the extinct German 3rd *Reich* a quarter of a century earlier. The other three tanks remained in Spain as gate guards at the barracks of the tank units.

The Israeli Army has preserved at least one *Panzer* IV captured to the Syrians, at the School of the Armoured Corps of the *Tsah Haganah Le Israel*. Another of the "Spanish" tanks is preserved in a German museum.

Chimeras

By early January 1944, six months before the Allied landings on the Normandy bea-

Two officers of the *Regimiento de Caballería «Farnesio» nº 12* (Valladolid) pose in front of the four *Panzer* IVs of the unit in 1958.

Colección Jesús García Campos

ches, even before the termination of the «*Bär*» Programme, and in the absence of the large amount of equipment signed with the German industry, the Spanish Government started some talks with Germany for the purchase of additional equipment as an extension of the programme in progress. As a result of several Spanish requests recorded in at least two notes and two coded telegrams sent to Berlin, the German Ambassador in Spain delivered a document to the Minister of Foreign Affairs dated 28 February that offered the possibility of acquiring assorted military equipment. Spanish official milieus began to talk about the new purchase programme under the codename «*Ankara*». The German Ambassador's offer considered a much smaller delivery than the «*Bär*» Programme, under the same five headings, namely communications, tanks, anti-aircraft equipment, aircraft and motorcycles[14].

The offer, as regards his department competences, was accepted by the Army Minister as an extension of the «*Bär*» Programme, keeping the same conditions established in the latter. As far

as the tanks were concerned, the negotiation totalled thirty-three *Panzer* IV tanks, including three command tanks, with the corresponding ammunition supplies..

Around that time, as a complement of the «*Ankara*» Programme[15], and through the chairman of AGEKA[16], Herr Eltze, the acquisition of another complementary consignment of military hardware was negotiated, comprised of sixty-seven type IV tanks, sixty 75-mm Rheinmetall guns, a 150/52 Rheinmetall gun and a 210-mm Skoda gun.

The addition of the thirty-three tanks of the «*Ankara*» and the sixty-seven of the «*Eltze*» programmes makes a total of one hundred new type IV tanks, badly needed by the newborn Spanish Armoured Division. For the negotiation, the Spanish Military Attaché in Berlin made a consultation regarding the intended organization of the 100 tanks asked for, so as to be in a position to specify which types and proportion of command tanks should be included. The colonel commanding the 5ª Sección of the Army General Staff, *coronel* Emilio Torrente, sent the 4ª Sección of that body a complete report to answer the questions posed by the Military Attaché in Berlin. *Coronel* Torrente, apart from answering Marín de Ber-

Two shots of the *Panzer* IV *Ausf H* of the *Regimiento de Caballería «Farnesio»* n° 12, going past the presiding platform on the commemoration of the 19th anniversary of the Nationalist victory in the Spanish Civil War at Valladolid.

Colección Jesús García Campos y Artemio Mortera

nardo's consultations in that curious report, so far unpublished, raised suggesting questions like "... *Are there plans to buy tanks heavier than the M-IV, such as the Tiger, or 50-mm gun tanks are going to be bought instead?*" and he continued "... *the tank battalion organization can be a mixed one, of light and medium tanks, if the current OB criteria are to be used... some countries even mix them up in companies. Should it be made up of two or three 50-mm gun companies and a 75-mm company, or two of each type? If Tiger tanks were bought, they could fit in the composition of a company of that type, and a further two companies of 75-mm gun tanks and one 50-mm. This has to be studied in detail...*".

The only certain thing in this affair is that the «Ankara» and «Eltze» programmes could not have seen fruition but in paper and in the wishes of the Spanish military; the hundred *Panzer* IV tanks, at hand's reach for more than one, never arrived in Spain, and the *Tigers* never roared...

---

1 As a matter of fact, no call of a German merchant vessel with such an important cargo was ever recorded either in the War Diary or other papers of the German Naval Attaché's office in Madrid.

2 Data from the "*Resumen general de necesidades de armamento (pie de paz)*", submitted by the *Sexta Sección del Estado Mayor del Ejército*, December 1942. These data were furnished to the *Comisión Extraordinaria para el Material de Guerra* and were used to evaluate the needs of the *Ejército de Tierra* regarding tanks. (General Martínez de Campos' Documents. Archivo Histórico Militar, Avila).

3 «Revista Española de Historia Militar», issue no 3, May/June 2000.

4 Might have been *Panzerkampfwagen* IIIs.

5 This corresponded to the *Panzerkampfwagen* IV.

6 The cost included the ammunition for the StuG III bat-

tery, 2,500 G.P. 7.5-cm mod. 39, 2,500 G.R. 7.5-cm mod. 34, 63,840 7.92-S.m.K. cartridges (half of them tracers), ten Z 85 destructor charges for engines and ten Z 72s for guns.

7 Sixteen twin 3.7-cm S.K. mounts with 16,000 shells, eight 2-cm quadruple *Flak* 38 gun mounts, twenty quadmount 2-cm *Flak* 38 guns and 20,000 3.7-cm shells for submarine *flak* guns.

8 Single price for each tank was 263,000 RM.

9 The tanks sold to Spain, chassis nos. 84,579 to 84,634, corresponded to the first ones in the series, which started at 84,401 and ended at 91,500. Three noticeable characteristics denote it, the rear idler wheel, identical to the G series, the return rollers with rubber bands and the lack of MG-34 mount in the tank commander cupola.

10 The former *Regimiento de Carros de Combate* nº 1, based at Campamento.

11 The former *Regimiento de Carros de Combate* nº 2, based in Seville.

12 As a matter of fact, budgets and purchase accounts were based on these data were established in the economic talks held in Madrid. Afterwards, a correction had to be made on the basis of the real figures, i.e. twenty tanks and ten assault guns.

13 Maybe a full company, with ten tanks. This is not confirmed.

14 These headings were extended as time went by.

15 One day we shall study in detail the aspects and negotiations that surrounded the failed *«Ankara»* Programme. Some would probably be surprised about the equipment discussed in the final stages of the negotiation. Here is an advance, twenty-five Steyr offroad command cars and *Nebelwerfer* rocket-launchers.

16 AGEKA: State Company for the Sale of German Military Equipment. The real name was a non-vowelled acronym A.G.K., although it is present in numerous period records in the vowelled form, including German and company records. Some historians make a mistake here by attributing the vowelled designation to Spanish ignorance. (García Pérez. «*Franquismo y Tercer Reich*»).

Exercises at the drill ground. A German *Panzer* IV poses with a Russian-made 45-mm anti-tank gun and an American Jeep Willys. Three different eras coexisted in the Spanish Army in the early fifties.

A.G.A., via J. M. Manrique

Spain restores a *Panzer* IV *Ausf H*

The story dates back to 2003, when the *Sección de Patrimonio* of the *Instituto de Historia y Cultura Militar* (IHCM) started a new strategy to make defence companies involved in the preservation tasks of the historical and cultural heritage of the *Ejército de Tierra*.

The restoration of the *Panzer* IV *Ausf H* is a testimony to the huge care of the SPA-MIR company in relation to the preservation of the heritage of the Spanish Army, as well as a good evidence of their technical and industrial capacity to carry out any project of this type, and of their disposition to take part in any activity in the field of the maintenance and reconstruction of heavy vehicles.

Roughly, the goal of the plan developed by the company was to make the over-60-year old tank –and more than forty as a gate guard– operational again, turn the turret and elevate the gun, a process after which it should be returned to the Army, who should keep it in working condition.

An imposing view of the *Panzer* IV *Ausf H* restored in Spain by the SPA-MIR company (Madrid) at the request of the *Instituto de Historia y Cultura Militar.*

Background

The restoration and public exhibition of the German *Panzer* IV *Ausf H* tank was born as a result of the talks held in late 2003 by *teniente coronel* Antonio Ocaña Ocaña and the *Sección de Patrimonio* of the Área General de Patrimonio of the IHCM.

The prearrangements of *teniente coronel* Ocaña, of the *División de Material* (DIMA) and the SPA-MIR company resulted, in January 2004, in a formal offer from Mr Domingo Rivera, General Manager of SPA-MIR, to the *General Director* of the IHCM to carry out the restoration of one of the three *Panzer* IVs preserved by the *Ejército.*

In the early days of February 2004, the IHCM declared this initiative as of top interest and designed the persons to make up the contact board by both sides for the matter.

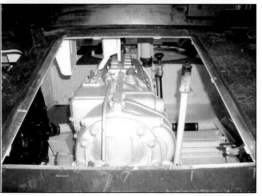

Four shots of the tank recently restored at the SPA-MIR facilities, Madrid..

In the weeks that followed, several meetings were held at the IHCM, and a draft plan for the restoration was made. Once discussed at further meetings, it materialized in the "Plan for the Restoration of a *Panzer* IV H".

The plan included a series of actions to be carried out that could be summed up as follows:
- Inspection of the tanks
- Technical Report for the restoration
- Report on the restoration managing
- Carrying out of the restoration
- Public exhibition of the restored tank

In order to establish which of the three *Panzer* IV H tanks in Spain was in the best condition for the restoration, permission was asked to carry out an inspection by the staff of the *Sección de Patrimonio* of the IHCM, along with a technical team of the SPA-MIR company.

The tanks were inspected at their respective locations at Santovenia de Pisuerga (Valladolid), Burgos and El Goloso (Madrid), on the 27, 28 and 29 April 2004. The tank at Santovenia was discarded for its poor condition and lack of engine, the one in the Tank Museum at El Goloso was selected for restoration, and the one at Burgos was proposed for spares. By mid-May the SPA-MIR company rendered the Technical Report on the condition of the three *panzers*.

Description of the work to be carried out
Once the project was approved, the 15 October 2004 *Boletín Oficial del Estado*[17] included the corresponding order to fund it and move the *Panzer* IV *Ausf H* from the Madrid and Burgos barracks to the Madrid SPA-MIR facilities for study and restoration.

The company then made the restoration plan to study the time and resources available and analyzed the locations and distribution of the works.

Next page top: The tank from the museum at El Goloso is hauled by a heavy crane onto a trailer, to be moved to the facilities of the rebuild company.
Next page bottom: Once at the SPA-MIR facilities, the tank was dismantled. It was in a sorrow condition.

Before and after the *Panzer* IV reconstruction, top to bottom: the right hatch of the turret, engine fans, instrument panel and transmission block, with the driving and gear levers. The results are obvious.

The workers assigned to the project had over twenty years' experience in the maintenance of military vehicles and were specialists for their respective tasks.

The main difficulties lay in the lack of knowledge of the real condition and decay of the tanks, as the prior inspection of the operational condition of the sub-assemblies was only visual.

The philosophy of the company to face such a representative project was always to keep the tank configuration as original as possible, although this might involve –as it actually happened– an additional workload in the equipment and sub-assemblies restoration. This effort was worthwhile as the final result was a vehicle fully restored according to the preservation guidelines of the military heritage.

The project phases were basically the same as in other full reconstruction projects in which SPA-MIR specializes, industrial activities to which it is skilfully suited:

- Document-tracing
- Strip-down
- Restoration of the sub-assemblies
- Re-assembly
- Final tests

Document tracing

The document-tracing phase started after the signing of the restoration agreement. The tank arrived at SPA-MIR with no reference documents. The company thus had to start research work, contacting military archives, tank museums, collectors and fans in Spain and abroad, proudly including this publishing house. An arduous task to compile original manuals, photos and articles related to the vehicle started, until enough documents were available to carry out the work. However, for a long part of the strip-down phase, not many documents were yet available, so some tasks were postponed to prevent wrong moves or damage to the equipment.

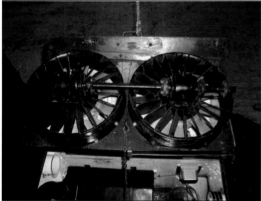

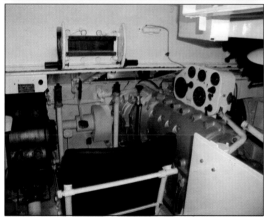

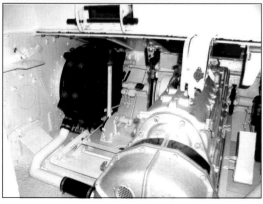

Strip-down

ABefore the workshop tasks started, other problems were the lack of spares, missing parts and sub-assemblies, along with the high degree of general deterioration, the corrosion of many parts and dirt that made it difficult to work in suitable conditions.

The strip-down phase was carried out along the logical sequence, starting with the turret, gun and casemate, then the engine bay and hull (interior) to be finished with the running gear.

Once removed from the tank, the sub-assemblies were stripped down and the list of equipment to repair was made.

Restoration

The next phase was the restoration of the sub-assemblies. It was based on the restoration of the original parts to keep the tank configuration as original as possible. In some cases, the replacement of some parts was indispensable, most of which had to be built using the old parts as patterns.

Only part of the screws and gaskets had to be replaced, mostly for security reasons. The sub-assemblies were finished when all the parts were repaired and were ready for final assembly in the tank, suitably repainted.

Reassembly and final tests

Once the sub-assemblies were rebuilt, they were fitted on the tank again in the reverse order with the priceless help of manuals and data obtained during the strip-down (diagrams and pictures).

The main engine and electric system assemblies could be tested before the final re-assembly. When the tank was finished, a series of functional tests and rectifications necessary for the tuning were carried out.

The final result

After nearly one year of strenuous hard work, a SPA-MIR team of workers headed by Alejandro González and made up of Luis Carmona de Alba, José Antonio Martín Rodríguez and Luis Martín Baides (fitters), Francisco Aguilar Encina (painter), José Ciudad Carranza (welder), Jaime Corrochano Gómez (motor engineer), Antonio Gutiérrez

Marcos (gun, turret ring and cupola) and Joaquín Urbano Luque (electrician), managed to make one of the most representative tanks of the Second World War, the *Panzer* IV *Ausf H,* roll again, with less warring illusions than sixty years earlier, but with the best effort for the preservation of the Spanish military heritage.

Several views of the rebuild of the water-cooled V 12 Maybach HL 120 TRM gasoline engine. On the next page, top, the engine is fitted back into its compartment.

The truth is that hearing the engine of this 25-ton steel monster roar and sitting at the commander's seat –as the writer has done– is an indescribable feeling, and certainly all tank fans will understand.

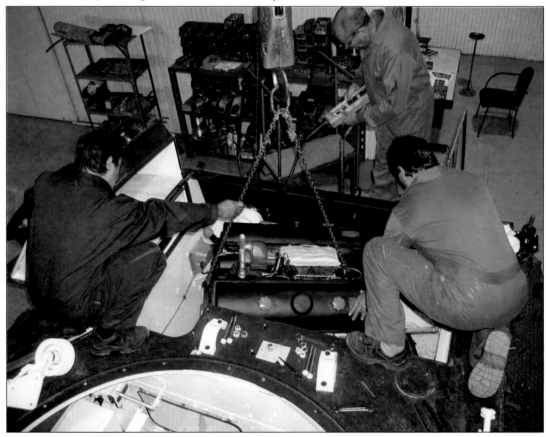

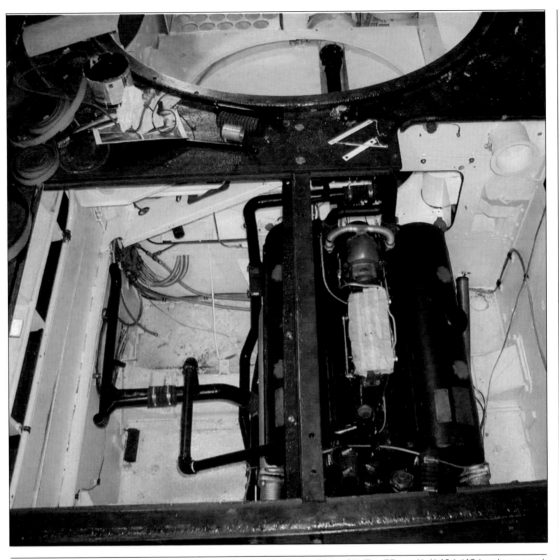

Bottom: two views of the breechblock of the gun fitted to the *Panzer* IV *Ausf H*. The 75-mm KwK-40 L/48 has been repaired and is fully functional, although the IHCM does not allow firing it.

We all sat at our places and the driver, with the obvious skill of one of the most remarkable workers in the restoration team, made the right track turn, with the left one at a stop, to go straight towards the way out and climb a quite

Three views of the *Panzer* IV *Ausf H* turret removed from its original place, before and after its reconstruction.

steep hill that would take us to the test ground. At the start of the climb, the tank hobbled and had to be stopped. On a shorter gear, the obs-

Several views of the re-assembly of the interior of the hull (driving and combat rooms). The work carried out by the SPA-MIR workers was always extremely careful, full of professionalism and know-how. It must be stressed that the work started out with not even a poor factory plan nor any sort of indications from a workshop foreman or something.

tacle was overcome. Once in the field, and after some power displays —gently, the Army is running short on spares–, we were able to photograph the tank minutely, sitting at all stations and touching anything we wanted to. To the last detail, everything runs smoothly.

The only black spot, if any, is the colour paint paintwork. It could have been painted khaki, the colour it wore in its whole life in the Spanish Army. Instead, it has been painted panzer grey, a colour the H type never wore. According to the company's PR, the *Instituto de Historia y Cultura Militar* takes all the blame for this unforgivable whim.

After two splendid hours, the time to say goodbye came. The tank turned back and headed for the wash yard; it should be returned to the state we found it, shining. When

we left SPA-MIR, the feeling was impressive. We were lucky; we had made one of every fan's dreams come true. We promised we would come back.

---

17 The Spanish Official Gazette, translator's note.

Top: final stages of the tank at the restoration hangar.

Centro: the open inspection hatch of the transmission and the final steps show an extremely rare image of the Panzer IV. Right, the identification plate of the tank denoting the H variant, with the turret number (85.596) and the hull chassis number (84.632).

Izquierda: Painting and final view of the Spanish *Panzer IV Ausf H*.

Next page: excellent view of the driver's seat of the rebuilt tank.

Painting and final view of the Spanish *Panzer IV Ausf H.*

ILLUSTRATIONS

44